WOODS ILLUSTRATED
ON ENDPAPERS

FRONT

ROSEWOOD	SATINWOOD
ENGLISH ELM	OAK
MAHOGANY	ASH

BACK

BIRCH	SCOTS PINE
WALNUT	BEECH
APPLEWOOD	YEW

THE OBSERVER'S
POCKET SERIES

.   .   .

THE OBSERVER'S BOOK
OF FURNITURE ∽ ∽

The Observer's Books

THE OBSERVER'S BOOK OF

FURNITURE

by
JOHN WOODFORDE

Illustrated by
ROY SPENCER

*Describing furniture from
Tudor to Victorian times,
with 195 line illustrations*

FREDERICK WARNE & CO. LTD.
FREDERICK WARNE & CO. INC.
LONDON   •   NEW YORK

© FREDERICK WARNE & CO. LTD.

LONDON, ENGLAND

1964

Reprinted 1966

© *Revised Edition* 1967

Reprinted 1970

LIBRARY OF CONGRESS CATALOG CARD NO.

64.18383

ISBN 0 7232 0077 7

Printed in Great Britain by
Butler & Tanner Ltd., Frome
1644.670

CONTENTS

PREFACE

THE examples have been grouped in the conventional periods and set out in this order: chests, chairs, tables, other living-room furniture, bedroom furniture. The main pages are supplemented by illustrations of woods and handles. There is a short glossary as well as an index.

The years given are rarely more than an indication of when a piece first became established in its place of origin—usually London. The bulk of surviving furniture corresponding to the drawings is of later date because of the time lag between the setting of a style and its adoption by country craftsmen.

Dating is sometimes made difficult by the practice, as prevalent in the 19th century as today, of reproducing the furniture of a previous century. Fakes are in a different category. With these an attempt has been made to persuade buyers that they are getting a valuable original. Only by experience can the difference in the patina, or surface, of such pieces be detected.

The author and publishers wish to thank Mr. J. F. Hayward of the Victoria and Albert Museum's Department of Woodwork for reading through the manuscript and making numerous valuable comments. The author wishes also to thank his wife for her help with the index and encouragement throughout the compiling of the book.

JOHN WOODFORDE

GLOSSARY

Antique. Up to the 19th century this meant classical, of ancient Greece or Rome. Now more usually furniture made before 1830.

Art Nouveau. Stiff, vertical furniture style at the turn of the 19th century.

Baluster. Pillar, usually turned, to support rail.

Baroque. Whimsical or grotesque style developed in the 17th century from Renaissance forms.

Beading. Small semi-circular moulding (ridge).

Bevel. Sloping edge given to a flat surface.

Cabinet-making. Craft of skilled joinery, using veneers.

Carpentry. Making of wooden structures by nailing timbers together.

Carver. The chair with arms, in a set for dining, to be used by the person carving.

Cornice. Upper projecting member on large piece of furniture.

Dentils. Series of small rectangular teeth as under-moulding of cornice.

Fillet. Small flat moulding, narrow strip.

Finial. Knob ornament finishing off post such as chair upright.

French Polish. Transparent gum made of Shellac dissolved in methylated spirit.

Gadrooning. Edging of carved, indentical, oval shapes.

Japanning. European imitation of Oriental glossy lacquer finish achieved by use of gum-lac dissolved in spirits.

Joinery. Work that has joints—dovetail, mortise and tenon, etc.

GLOSSARY (continued)

Marquetry. Inlaying of patterns made by various woods, etc., into veneer.

Mortise. Hole cut in a timber to make joint with another having shaped piece, or tenon, to fit hole.

Moulding. Ornamental band, usually raised. Numerous varieties.

Ogee. Shape of a support (or moulding): concave below and convex above.

Ormolu. Derived from French for ground gold. Gilded metal mounts.

Patera. Classical round or oval disc stuck on or carved.

Patina. Colour and feel that wood takes on as a result of age, wear and polishing.

Pediment. Ornamental structure surmounting cornice of cabinets, bookcases, etc.

Plinth. Low, usually square, base of a piece of furniture.

Reeding. Decoration with a series of slim pipes, or reeds. Now especially associated with the Regency period.

Rococo. Asymmetrical, florid decoration based on rocks and shells. Prevalent in Europe 1730–80.

Splat. Upright member in the middle of the back of a chair.

Stretcher. Horizontal bar joining legs of furniture.

Turning. Working wood by applying cutting tools to it as it rotates on a lathe.

Veneer. Thin sheet of hard timber glued on a solid article to give an elegant finish.

HANDLES

Handles and their backplates vary greatly in points of detail, but the following examples represent the main types. In examples 1 to 6 the handle part is held by a metal strip, or strips, bent outwards at the back on the paper-fastener principle. Numbers 7 and 8 show the first use of drilled bolt heads for receiving the ends of the handle. Numbers 1 to 3 are iron, the rest brass except for 23 and 24.

1.
Tudor to
early Stuart.
Drop

2.
Tudor to
early Stuart.
Loop

3.
Early Stuart

4.
Mid- to late
17th century.
Pear drop

5.
William and
Mary.
Split tail

6.
William and
Mary—and up
to mid-18th
century on less
fashionable
pieces

7.
William and
Mary. Ring

8.
Early Queen
Anne.
Solid
backplate

9.
Late Queen
Anne. Pierced
backplate.

10.
Early
Georgian.
Elaborately
pierced
backplate

11.
Mid-Georgian

12.
Mid- to late
Georgian.
Plain loop

13.
Mid-Georgian.
French
influence

14.
Mid-Georgian.
Chinese
influence

15.
Mid-Georgian
to 1800

16.
Mid- to late
Georgian

17.
Late Georgian.
Stamped

18.
Late Georgian.
Ring

19.
Late Georgian.
Stamped

20.
Late Georgian
and Regency.

21.
Regency to
William IV.
Lion mask
with ring

22.
Early
Victorian—
and up to 1900

23.
Early to
mid-Victorian.
Porcelain

24.
Victorian.
Wood.
Also late
Georgian

A Tudor Interior c. 1550

TUDOR PERIOD
1485—1603

NEARLY all Tudor furniture was made of oak and tended to be heavy and uncomfortable, though seats would be softened here and there with a cushion. The better pieces were carved according to the contemporary style in architecture. Often they were gilded and gaily painted; this helped to protect them against damp air let in by unglazed windows and against insect-ridden rushes. The painting continued into the early 17th century when standards of comfort improved.

The year 1485 and the crowning of Henry VII officially marks the close of the Middle Ages, but the Tudor house and its fittings remained austerely mediaeval. For much of the period little furniture existed, even the big houses making do with bed, bench, stool, table and chest. Chairs were used only by the master and mistress of the house as they presided over their household gathered for meals in the hall.

Early Tudor furniture can still be seen in museums and churches and occasionally in old country houses. Chests especially have survived; large boxes have always been made in quantity for dry storage, and in Tudor times they served as seats and tables and even as beds.

Furniture production increased in Henry VIII's reign and new types were evolved. The main boost was a spurt in private-house building. On the proceeds of dissolving the monasteries the King built palaces (which impressed foreigners); his friends converted religious establishments into country seats; wool and other merchants put up sturdy residences.

The practice of proper joinery had now ousted weighty plank construction and furniture was easier to move about. Panelling for walls became popular; chests pushed up against it gave the inspiration for free-standing, panelled settles. The carved ornament of this time sometimes shows the influence of the Renaissance, already well established in Italy, which was spread slowly by imported examples and by Italian craftsmen living in England. Garlands and profile heads in roundels, often crudely adapted, were freely mixed with the traditional Gothic linenfold and Tudor Rose and arch designs.

By the end of Queen Elizabeth's reign domestic interiors presented a scene very different from that when Henry VII came to the throne. The Elizabethans built, or enlarged, to a sophisticated plan. The hall, now less important and only one storey high, left space for other rooms. The long gallery came into being. It was used for music and dancing and a display of portraits that were sometimes said to be ancestral when they were not.

However, the newly rich owners of these houses grossly overdid the decoration. They encouraged the carvers to add ideas from Flemish and German pattern books to their only partially understood repertoire of Italian classical designs. As a result, the plain linenfold panelling of mid-Tudor times tended to give way to industrious chiselling on any bare surface of wall and furniture. Favourite motifs were medallions, lozenges, eagles, naked boys and festoons of fruit. The strap-work decoration and the bulbous swelling of table legs were of Flemish origin.

Among the places where Tudor furniture is to be seen are Hatfield House, Hertfordshire; Red Lodge, Bristol; Hardwick Hall, Chesterfield and Shakespeare's Birthplace, Stratford-on-Avon.

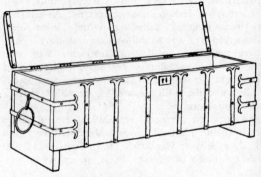

Plank Chest 15th century

The chest remained for centuries the most important piece of furniture. It served as seat and table as well as a dry place for keeping things. A lighter, leather-covered sort was called a coffer. The chest here is the work of a carpenter who probably knew nothing about mortise and tenon joints—and who had received no instructions about tracery decoration. His box is made of hewn planks strapped together with iron bands, the top attached by wire staples linked together to make hinges. Iron locks were invariably fitted. The base is raised above the ground by having the sides lower than the front and back. Late mediaeval chests have been preserved through becoming at some stage church property.

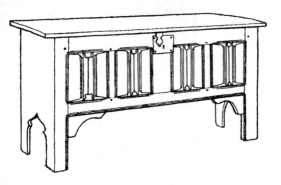

Joined Chest c. 1530

The craft of joinery was established by the 16th century—a big step forward—and chests had a framework of morticed rails and stiles held by oak pins and grooved for panels. The hinged staple for use with the lock served as a handle for lifting the lid. The linenfold pattern often carved on the panels originated on the Continent.

The joiners' panel and frame method is still widely used. It is comparatively light, and allows for movement of the wood, the panels not being rigidly fixed in their grooves.

Chests did not acquire drawers till the middle of the 17th century.

B

Wainscot Chair c. 1530

A contemporary name. Such chairs were always described as 'joyned' to distinguish the work of joiners from that of mere carpenters. The box-like form clearly shows how early chairs developed out of the chest. A locker beneath the seat was usual.

The example has the linenfold panels typical of Tudor craftsmanship. There is also one panel carved in the Renaissance manner. The chair would have been used in the hall by the master of the house only; everyone else sat on forms or stools. Chairs did not come into general use till the next century.

18

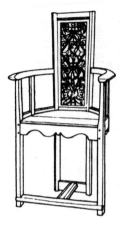

Caquetoire c. 1540

A less ponderous type of joined chair that was
occasionally made in the 16th century for important people. It is based on a French type, the name
'caquetoire' coming from its use as a conversation
chair. The example drawn here is in the Victoria
and Albert Museum. Its good state of preservation
may have something to do with the fact that when
found in Devon in the 19th century it was covered
in numerous coats of black paint. The detail of
the Renaissance carving on the back is still sharp,
and it can be seen that the female bust set in a
lozenge is wearing the clothes of about 1535.

Turned Chair Late 16th century

Tudor craftsmen were familiar with the processes of turning with a pole lathe. Three-legged 'thrown' chairs, a traditional mediaeval type, persisted well into the 17th century. Suggesting bundles of pastry, they were at least easily portable. In the mid-18th century they came to be associated romantically with the Gothic ages. Horace Walpole wanted some for his Gothic Revival house, Strawberry Hill, and wrote to ask a friend to search in Cheshire. His description: 'The seats are triangular, the backs, arms and legs loaded with turnery.'

Elizabethan Joined Chair c. 1600

An elaborately carved and inlaid example of the chair that succeeded the wainscot chair. Several chairs of this type would probably have been found in a gentleman's house by the end of the 16th century. The rectangular framing remains, but the space below the seat is no longer enclosed by panels. The front supports are baluster-turned and rise above the seat to carry sloping arms. Scrolled brackets, or earpieces, on either side of the back became a usual extra piece of decoration. The low front stretcher was useful for keeping one's feet off the floor rushes.

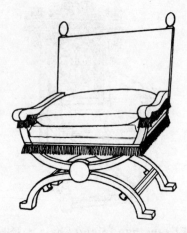

Elizabethan X-Chair c. 1600

Old inventories and illustrated manuscripts show
that the X-framed, folding chair was not unusual
in the houses of the rich at the time of Henry VIII.
Early examples survive in York Minster and Win-
chester Cathedral. A chair with a history of use
by royalty, it was the first to depend on textile
coverings in an age of ungarnished oak. The seat
was a cradle of webbing which took a squab cushion.
Under James I, upholstered furniture was to
become popular in the big houses.

Glastonbury c. 1600

A term for a type of chair with a folding framework said to be based on a chair associated with the last Abbot of Glastonbury (d. 1539). Pieces of similar shape have been made from time to time ever since, and the elderly examples seen in country churches are nearly always of 19th century make.

One notes the carefully elbowed arms. Until late in the 16th century all chairs had arms. When single chairs came to be made they were thought of as stools with backs and were known as 'back stools'.

23

Box Settle c. 1600

The chest was commonly used for sitting on. Giving it arms and a back (panelled as walls were) added still further to its usefulness. In winter the resultant settle would be turned to face the fire, its high back warding off the draught. If two or three settles were to hand, they would be used to form a snug little room within a room. Screens had not been thought of in Tudor England.

Of mediaeval origin, settles continued to be made for farmhouses and kitchens till well into the 19th century. They are sometimes seen fixed to the wall in large old fireplaces.

Milking Stool Late 16th century

The fitting of a back to this primitive stool reveals
it as an ancestor of the equally simple Windsor
chair that began to be made by wheelwrights and
turners at the end of the 17th century. The basic
structure is the same: a solid block of wood with
holes drilled in it for stick legs and back. Sometimes the ends of the sticks were heated before
being driven in so that they swelled on cooling and
fitted tighter. The three-legged stool was a
humble article; the rectangular, four-legged stool
with pinned joints was distinguished from it by the
name 'joyned stool'.

25

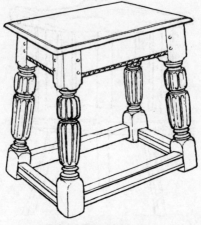

Joined Stool c. 1590

A joiner-made article that was used freely all over the house in Elizabethan and Jacobean times. Its immediate predecessor had solid, or slab, supports instead of four baluster legs. Joined stools often matched the dining table in construction and carving. They would be stacked beneath it when not in use.

The legs of this type were invariably linked at the base by the familiar low stretchers on which sitters liked to rest their feet free of the ground. The rushes and other objects strewn about the hall floor were inclined to be unwholesome.

Trestle Table c. 1500

The Tudor hall was used for several purposes besides dining, and often only the master's high table at one end would stay permanently in position. The trestle tables, round which sat dependants and servants in the body of the hall, were designed to take to pieces easily for stacking.

A table of the sort illustrated consisted of a large board,* or boards, which merely rested on the uprights, or trestles, as they are called; these were linked by a rail held in position with oak pegs.

* Hence the phrase 'board and lodging'.

27

Draw Table c. 1550

An early kind of space-saving extending table which was made in large numbers. Its length is almost doubled by pulling out the two under leaves, mounted on slanting bearers, until the top leaf is able to drop into the space between them leaving a level surface. It remained a popular type until the 1620s or later and has been reproduced in modern times.

The example has a Gothic-shaped underframing with chamfered edges. The slab-ended bench in front would probably have been considered 'en suite'. By the next century benches had acquired legs.

28

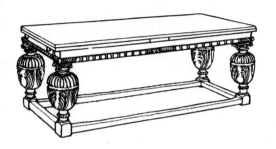

Elizabethan Draw Table c. 1580

A massive table incorporating the draw-leaf device. The bulbous swelling of cup-and-cover form on each turned leg, with Ionic capital above, reflects the Elizabethans' love for imposing ornament on furniture. The leg design was of Flemish origin.

All kinds of long oak tables are often called refectory tables, but historians deride the term as dealers' jargon. Monasteries and their refectories were dissolved, they point out, by 1539 and it cannot be thought that any obtainable table once stood in a monastic dining-room. However, the word carries too agreeable an idea of jolly monks lingering over their wine to make it easy to abandon.

Close Cupboard c. 1540

In mediaeval and Tudor times the word cupboard, variously spelt, normally meant either a single board for putting cups and jugs on or a piece with open shelves. But cupboards with doors *were* made and called close cupboards and, later, presses.

The carving on the upper part of this one shows the influence of the Italian Renaissance; carved heads in roundels (Romayne work) was a form of decoration introduced at the beginning of the 16th century. The background for an obviously rich piece of this sort would probably have been oak-panelled walls draped here and there with hangings of tapestry.

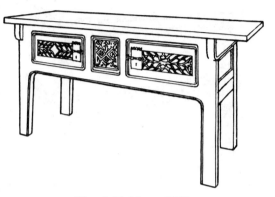

Hutch Table c. 1530

Smaller-doored containers were known as hutches. The word comes from the French 'huche' (in which form it appears in the *Paston Letters*) meaning a chest or a meal tub.

This hutch on legs is a superior article with its carving of Gothic tracery patterns. As the top would have been used as a resting place for cups and jugs, it was probably also thought of as a cup-board in the original sense of the word.

To protect them against the weather—there was no glass for windows—such pieces were often painted. Gay colours were chosen.

Elizabethan Court Cupboard c. 1590

A traditional open-shelved cup-board for holding
and displaying cups and plate, 'court' meaning
short (French); also called a buffet cupboard. This
one is inlaid with chequer patterns in woods other
than oak and has oblique gadrooning round the
cornice. The frieze beneath the middle shelf is the
front of a drawer.

Forerunners of the dresser and sideboard, these
pieces continued fashionable till the middle of the
17th century. Some had a secret shelf for valuables
in the space below the top, reached by groping
underneath.

Bible Box c. 1580

A small joined box with dolphin-like scrolls on the
front and a stout iron lock. The collector's term
'Bible box' is often suspect when applied to containers of this sort. The majority of them were not
made for a Bible, but for the safe keeping of docu-
ments, books, small articles of dress and valuables.

Developments were boxes with a drawer at the
bottom and boxes with a sloping lid. (See the next
page.)

C

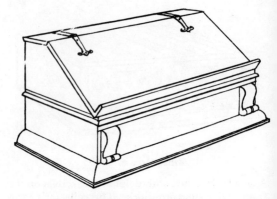

Desk Box c. 1590

Portable desks began to be made when printed books, articles of great value, became procurable. They were still being made in a variety of elegant styles in the 19th century. The Duke of Wellington wrote despatches from the field of battle on a box very similar to the example. It is on show at Apsley House, London.

Originally, however, the slope of the hinged lid was designed for laying out a book for reading rather than for writing purposes, although writing equipment would be stored inside, along with a book or two. Later desk boxes developed legs, or were put on stands, and became independent pieces of furniture.

Elizabethan Posted Bed c. 1600

Under the Tudors most people slept on straw or on straw contained in a shallow box, but plenty of more advanced bedsteads with canopies had existed for the rich since the Middle Ages. At first the canopy and its curtains were attached to the ceiling. When posted bedsteads with built-in tester began to be made early in the 16th century the curtains became part of the structure. Within the four posts—or, as was usual, four posts and a back—stood the bed frame itself, cord stretched across holding the mattress. Beds for the fashionable grew increasingly consequential.

35

STUART PERIOD
1603—1714

EARLY Stuart fashionable furniture, sturdy, insular and still oaken, kept most of the Elizabethan characteristics, but ornament became gradually less arbitrary and prominent. The reigns of James I and his cultured son, Charles I, saw certain advances in domestic comfort: increased use of padded upholstery, for example, and of carpets instead of rushes as a floor covering. It was a period of steady progress in the art of living, and of Palladian architecture by Inigo Jones that was well ahead of its time; it ended abruptly in 1642 with the outbreak of war between king and parliament.

Austerity and destruction marked the next twenty years, and all building and furnishing was curtailed. In general, the furniture made under the Protectorate had a severe, angular look; the Puritans liked the style of the farmhouse.

The Restoration of the monarchy in 1660 brought an extreme reaction. Back in England, Charles II and his exiled court surrounded themselves with furniture resembling the most lavish they had seen in France and Holland. The Continental taste of the Court spread over London, and the furniture that replaced losses in the Great Fire of 1666 was altogether lighter and more

A Restoration Interior c. 1680

elegantly finished. Chairs developed in a short time from mere seats into floridly carved ornamental pieces. Carving was greatly admired at this time; its best exponent, Grinling Gibbons, specialised in fruit and flowers in high relief.

Much of the first grade London furniture was made by immigrant craftsmen such as Dutchmen and Huguenot refugees—the Court cabinet-maker Gerreit Jensen was Dutch. Their standard of skill was high; they introduced the technique of veneering, already established on the Continent, and gilding, marquetry and lacquer. Home-made glue began to be used for joints. Walnut now succeeded oak as the fashionable wood for furniture and remained supreme until it gave place to mahogany about seventy years later. Beech, however, was used widely for chairs.

Improved joinery and fresh forms of decoration coincided with the invention of new types. An obvious example is the day bed, with adjustable end, often supplied to match a set of chairs. Small tables were developed for all kinds of sophisticated purposes, and so were stands, cabinets and cupboards. Looking-glasses came into general use, often in conjunction with the now popular chest of drawers.

Furniture of the William and Mary period was strongly and beneficially influenced by the Dutch cabinet makers who came to England with the King and worked for him at Hampton Court and Kensington Palace. The most noticeable of the features from Holland are curved, tied stretchers for chairs, and bonnet, or domed, tops for cabinets.

By the time of Queen Anne (1702–1714) English craftsmen had acquired a mature skill and ingenuity. It reveals itself today when repairs have to be done. Foreign techniques were mastered and furniture in a distinct English style had emerged, its chief characteristic the cabriole leg. Gentle, well proportioned and useful, it suited the Wren-style houses being built as happily as the style of these suited the soft unspoiled English countryside.

Among the places where Stuart furniture is to be seen are Hampton Court; Knole, Kent; Ham House, Richmond; Hatfield House, Hertfordshire; Lyme Park, Stockport; Cotehele House, Cornwall; Areton Manor, Isle of Wight and Levens Hall, Kendal.

Mule Chest c. 1640

A traditional lidded chest fitted at the bottom with
two drawers, which were then known as tills or
drawing boxes. Although invented in the first half
of the 17th century, it is generally considered a
Cromwellian article. The drawered chest went on
being made in the country till the mid-18th century; but in fashionable circles it soon developed
into the chest of drawers. The unsatisfactory term,
mule, in the sense of hybrid, was suggested later
on by its having the characteristics of two pieces
of furniture.

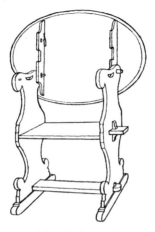

Table Chair c. 1615

A combination piece known as early as the late
16th century. Since nearly all existing specimens
were made in the 17th century, and well after the
Dissolution of the Monasteries, the modern term
monk's bench can be misleading.

A hinged, usually rounded back is designed to
swing over and lie on the arms to form a small
table. Oak pins hold it in position. Like the chest,
the table chair was often a portmanteau article, the
sort with a box seat serving also as a container.

41

Farthingale Chair c. 1620

A single chair, or 'back stool', with a high broad
seat and a low padded back with a strong rake to
it. The chair is said to have been designed to
accommodate and display to advantage women's
farthingales—dresses hooped with whalebone.
These had reached exaggerated proportions at the
court of James I.

Rather plain legs and straight stretchers were
usual for these chairs, but the upholstery was
handsomely embroidered. The term farthingale
chair seems to have been invented in Victorian
times.

Carver Chair c. 1650

A type of rush-seated armchair of which plenty
were made in the period 1650–1750. Dutch origin
seems likely since it appears in early paintings of
humble Dutch rooms. The legs rise as framing
posts behind and in front and are crowned with
finials. Spindles in the back and other points of
construction show the chair to be a fore-runner
of the Lancashire spindle back.

The name is an American thought and refers to
John Carver, an Englishman, who became the first
governor of the Plymouth Colony (1620), and who
is alleged to have taken the prototype of the chair
with him in the *Mayflower*.

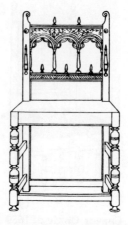

Derbyshire Chair c. 1650

Wooden-seated chairs like this were made in quantity in the period of roughly 1640–75. The type is associated with Yorkshire and Lancashire almost as much as with Derbyshire.

A cross rail with an arcading of ornamental spindles has been taken up as an alternative to the half-panelled back. The straight uprights end in scrolls. Split spindles glued to the surface of uprights were a common decoration; so were acorn-like knobs. Fussy and forbidding though this chair may seem, it has often been reproduced in modern times.

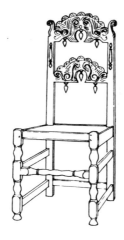

Mortuary Chair c. 1650

A once common variety of the mid-17th century Derbyshire (or Yorkshire) chair. The example has a slightly sunken seat for holding a cushion.

The term mortuary—that is, 'relating to death' —has come into use as a result of 19th century romanticism. The fictitious story went about that the moustached masks on the curved back rails portrayed the head of Charles I, who was executed in 1649.

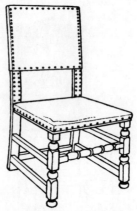

Cromwellian Chair c. 1655

The most representative piece of Commonwealth furniture, this chair reflects the Puritan tastes of the period (though the type went on being made in the reign of Charles II). The chunky oak frame has two pieces of leather stretched over it and held in place by brass-headed nails. The result is only fairly comfortable, as anyone will know who has sat on reproductions in 'old world' public houses.

Utility chairs of this sort were in general use by Cromwell's time. Upholstery and carving were then frowned on. But turning was for some reason acceptable, and front legs and stretcher were almost invariably bobbin-turned.

Early Cane Chair c. 1665

Weight-saving split cane was introduced from the Continent shortly after 1660, the year of the Restoration, and soon became a usual covering. At first the mesh was conspicuously wide.

Early cane chairs were similar in shape to the leather-covered Cromwellian ones; but the adoption of Continental twist-turning instead of bobbin-turning marked a break with tradition. For the new process, walnut was found a more amenable wood than oak. The barley sugar twist, as it is sometimes called, was now so much admired that craftsmen unable to adjust their lathes were prepared to cut the spirals by hand.

Charles II Chairs c. 1675 and 1685

Restoration chairs were exuberant. The Flemish S-scroll, flanking the back panel of the chair on the left, was often mixed with twist-turning in various flamboyant forms. The front stretcher would match the cresting rail.

The chair on the right shows the end-of-reign development of fixing the cresting on top of the raked uprights instead of between them. Arms for this type of chair were rounded, scrolled over their supports and dipped in the middle. Already tall, backs grew even taller in the reign of William and Mary.

Carolean Day Bed c. 1685

Caned day beds became a Court fashion in the Restoration period; it was a fashion which spread to large houses all over the country. Day beds were carved in the style of contemporary chairs, the head piece resembling the back of a chair, and were normally walnut, or beech painted black.

The day bed was the forerunner of the chaise-longue and the sofa. With a mattress and a cushion or two, it could be made reasonably comfortable for an after-dinner nap. The example shows an early form of the paw foot. Scroll feet were more usual at the time.

Marot Curved-back c. 1715

Chairs with undulating backs (seen from the side) were introduced at the end of the century. Uprights containing a single vertical splat had a bulge at the bottom to support the sitter's back and an inward curve towards the top to allow for the shoulders. A type of cabriole leg was now used, based on French and Italian examples. To accentuate the suggestion of an animal's hind leg it was often given a hoofed foot. Stretchers looked incongruous with such legs and were soon discarded.

The finely carved chair above represents a type favoured by Daniel Marot, a French Huguenot designer in the service of William III.

Queen Anne Chair c. 1710

The tallness of the back, and the cabriole legs, mark the transition between the William and Mary and the Queen Anne styles. The plain design of this chair encouraged production by country cabinet-makers. The example here, with front and back legs similar, appears a country piece from the unsure joinery of the top rail, the form of which demands it should overlap the uprights, and by a lack of delicacy in the fashioning of the back legs. In the provinces, beech or oak were used for imitating London walnut pieces.

51

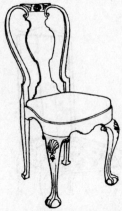

Queen Anne Chair c. 1715

A typical example of the walnut chair known as Queen Anne. Although the type was being made before Queen Anne died, most of these chairs date from George I's reign. The main features are the fiddle-shaped splat in a hooped, curving back; drop-in seat; unstretchered cabriole legs that are not quite round in section; ball and claw feet; scallop shell decoration. Back legs, at first square, as in the drawing, were later rounded all the way up and given pad feet.

The best chairs had burr walnut veneer on the curved seat frame and over the whole back. Matching armchairs had arms set back to allow for women's dresses.

52

Queen Anne Grandfather Chair c. 1710

A sentimental, late-Victorian label for a winged easy chair, and one that seems to have been inspired by the term grandfather clock for long case clocks. This was adopted as a result of the popular 1878 song beginning: 'My grandfather's clock was too large for the shelf, so it stood ninety years on the floor ... .' Plenty of high-backed grandfather chairs were made in the Queen Anne period. The needle-worked upholstery closely followed the lines of the wooden structure beneath. For substantial chairs of this sort, stretchers were found necessary until shorter cabriole legs were introduced.

William and Mary Stool c. 1690

Despite an increasing production of single chairs,
stools were still a familiar and important article of
furniture in late 17th century interiors. Even in
the houses of the nobility they would be the usual
seat for meals.

The art of carving was highly valued in the post-
Restoration period and stools were fashioned with
as much loving care and feeling for display as the
chairs. They were customarily made *en suite* with
these and the tables. Scrolling similar to that of the
legs and front stretcher of the stool drawn (this
one is upholstered in velvet) can be seen on the
chairs on page 48.

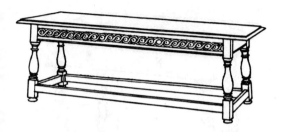

Jacobean Long Table c. 1625

Dining tables of the Jacobean period—that is, the reign of James I, 1603–25—were as massive as their predecessors, and built to last. Plenty have survived. The amount of carved ornament was now reduced and the Elizabethan melon bulbs on the legs were growing steadily less pronounced. Most legs were baluster-turned, as shown above. Tables were often extremely long, and those with fixed tops might have as many as eight legs. The wood was usually oak, though elm and yew were used.

William and Mary Side Table c. 1680

A popular design for side tables. A drawer was
fitted tight under a top now often decorated with
floral marquetry. Stretchers for tables, chairs and
other pieces were made in a distinctive curving
manner at this period—for reasons of appearance
rather than strength. They might run from leg to
leg, but more often they ran diagonally, as here,
forming either a knob or a small circular shelf in
the middle.

Twist-turning for legs was so well thought of
that country craftsmen lacking equipment would
sometimes simulate the form by cutting rectangular
legs in a curved profile.

Early Gate-leg c. 1650

A type which appeared at the beginning of the 17th
century and was called a falling table. The arrangement that allowed these tables to be shut together
and put against a wall quickly won approval, especially for smaller rooms. The earlier space-saver,
the draw table, was outmoded before the middle of
the century. The gate-leg table has a long history.

The early oak example here is perhaps uncom-
mon in having only two legs (reel-and-bobbin-
turned) to support the central, immobile section;
the gates on either side are set on the trestle base.
Nails hold the iron hinges of the flaps, while elsewhere joints are secured by oak pins, or dowels.

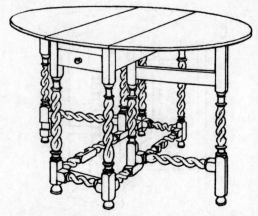

**Charles II or William and Mary Gate-leg
c. 1690**

Gate-leg tables were made in a variety of designs
and woods throughout the century. They were
used for meals (the dining room at Ham House
contained eight) and many had four gates.

The sort most often made had two gates, giving
a total of eight legs, and a round or oval top. The
drawing shows a typical late 17th century version,
solid walnut, with drawer and nearly all members
twist-turned in the post-Restoration manner, the
upright spirals bounded by vase forms. Hand-filed
screws now replaced nails for holding the flap
hinges.

James II Dresser c. 1685

A typical kitchen dresser of early type, a development of the Elizabethan court or buffet cupboard. It has four legs, the two in front baluster-turned, and three stretchers. The three drawer fronts are each decorated with a couple of 'panels', as was the custom with drawers at the time. The upper shelf is topped by a primitive scalloped design.

Dressers were often found adequate without the shelved upper section. The back board of this section is nearly always, by the way, a later addition.

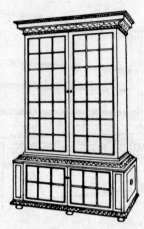

Pepysian Bookcase 1666

The free-standing bookcase, or press, as an alternative to fixed open shelves, was a mid-17th century development. In 1666 the diarist Samuel Pepys wrote of engaging 'Sympson, the Joyner' to make 'presses in which to set books now growing numerous'. The drawing shows one of twelve now housed at Magdalene College, Cambridge.

It is finely made of solid oak. The glass doors of upper and lower stages are subdivided by heavy glazing bars. There is a carved frieze under the boldly jutting-out cornice.

Bureau on Stand c. 1690

The traditional desk box first developed into an independent piece of furniture in the Restoration period (1660–1688). The sloping front of the example, walnut and about thirty inches wide, is hinged to fall forward on lopers, or slides. Within is a central well and a number of small drawers. The stand, with its curved stretchers, is typical of the William and Mary style for such structures.

The production of furniture for writing at was given a boost by the introduction of a national postal service: the first postmaster general, or 'master of the posts', was appointed in 1657.

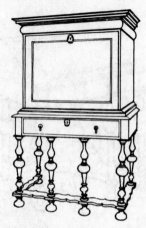

Escritoire on Stand c. 1690

Walnut or marquetry writing cabinets on stands
were developed at about the same time as bu-
reaux on stands, and remained popular till Queen
Anne's day. The tall fronts, supported by brass
elbow-jointed stays, disclose numerous beautifully
made small drawers and pigeon holes and secret
compartments.

These pieces, then called 'scrutoirs', were very
similar, when shut, to the marquetry cabinets of
the period with the upper stage enclosed by a pair
of doors. The term secretaire is now usually
reserved for the sort of desk that resembles a
straight-fronted chest of drawers.

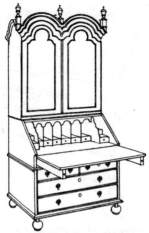

William and Mary Bureau Cabinet c. 1685

By the 1680s the bureau box was being attached
to a bun-footed chest of drawers instead of a stand.
The bureau in almost the form familiar today had
been evolved. Higher rooms encouraged the
elaboration of placing a cabinet on top. The one
here, pigeon-holed for papers and books, has the
double-hooded top and finials of Holland. The
arched doors are fitted with the new Vauxhall
mirror plate with wide flat bevels, giving the piece
a slightly coarse appearance. On cabinets for porcelain and ornaments the doors were soon to become
clear-glazed.

Queen Anne Bureau c. 1715

The walnut-veneered bureau on bracket feet, free
of cabinets, is one of the most satisfying pieces of
furniture introduced at the end of Queen Anne's
reign. The type was made throughout the century.

Behind the flap (at an angle of 45°) lie small
drawers, pigeon-holes and a central cupboard and,
very likely, a covered well and a few secret compartments. The drawers are oak-lined and have
dust boards between them. The applied moulding round the upper part of the carcase is a sur-
vival from older practice; it marks what would
have been the joint between the bureau box and
the chest it rested on.

Charles II Chest of Drawers c. 1660

Introduced in the middle of the 17th century. The basic form at that time has not been improved upon. Soon after the Restoration (1660) oak chests of drawers began to be made in large numbers. Some were inlaid with pieces of bone, ivory and mother-of-pearl. In the plain specimen above, much reproduced as 'Jacobean' in late Victorian times, what appear to be eight drawers are really four long ones: it was a favourite practice to have simulated panels on a single drawer to make it look like two. Central keyholes spoil the trick.

The example has been given 18th century bracket feet to replace the bun type.

William and Mary Chest of Drawers on Stand
c. 1690

The use of veneer on a base of oak or deal, or both, changed the appearance of chests of drawers. Panelled drawer fronts disappeared. By the end of Charles II's reign (1685) the better chests were raised on drawered stands with either baluster or, as above, spirally turned legs. The top drawers immediately beneath a brief cornice, were easily reached—unlike those of the tallboy to come. Rounded moulding was applied to the framework in front but not yet to the edges of the drawers. The drawing is of a walnut-veneered piece: many were covered with marquetry or japanned.

Queen Anne Bachelor Chest c. 1720

Equipped with either a writing slide or, as here, a hinged top flap, bachelor chests are low enough to be comfortably used as tables while sitting down. The name is modern and presumably relates to the usefulness of these small pieces of furniture in the bedroom of the single man.

Large numbers of homely but dignified chests of drawers were produced in Queen Anne's reign. The typical chest, as serviceable today as then, was straight-fronted and had four drawers. Walnut was the main wood for veneering—on top of oak for the best work. The sides were often left plain.

67

Queen Anne Dressing Table c. 1710

A walnut-veneered side table with drawers and knee recess and the early form of the cabriole leg. Three drawers were usual for holding the materials for painting and rougeing used by both men and women. A decorative dressing-table box to go on top might provide extra space for these things, and for brushes and combs. Looking-glasses on stands, the base of which was often a nest of miniature drawers, were now beginning to be made as separate units for standing on a dressing table or on an ordinary chest of drawers.

GEORGIAN PERIOD
1714—1800

THE word Georgian has become synonymous with well-designed. The high standard of 18th century furniture, even the screws of which were made by hand, was largely the result of a widespread liking for architecture based on the Greek and Roman rules of correct proportion. Cabinet-makers had to match the serenity and charm of the new buildings and took guidance from the architects or from the numerous pattern books published.

Everything favoured the making of pleasing furniture. It was an age of classical educations and grand tours of Europe; and scattered over Britain lived rich men with the leisure and inclination to study the best and insist on getting it. The example of what they ordered for their houses set a national standard of taste which showed itself in cottage as well as mansion.

Furniture design was nevertheless far from static in the Georgian period. Early in George I's reign attempts were made to improve on the gentle, domestic Queen Anne style; furniture was given more elaborate pediments and sturdier cabriole legs. Marked changes of fashion were brought by the introduction of mahogany (from Cuba and Honduras) which followed repeal of heavy import

A Georgian Interior c. 1780

duties in 1721. Cabinet-makers liked the close-grained new wood, which is harder and crisper than walnut and not attacked by worm, and found that it lent itself to the trying out of alternative forms. Mahogany was entirely suitable for the grand pieces in demand for the tall state rooms and libraries of Palladian houses.

Some of the grandest were designed by William Kent. His Italianate style was the style of architecture itself: Kent furniture looks as if it could have been carved out of stone as easily as wood. However, the ornate pieces suited the particular houses (Houghton and Holkham, for example) for which they were designed as an integral part.

In the middle of the century there was a craze for the undulating Louis XV style and furniture grew less heavily architectural. Designers developed an English version of French rococo. Thomas Chippendale's *The Gentleman and Cabinet-maker's Director*, 1754, helped to publicise the 'French' styles. It also drew furniture-makers' attention to a mid-century society taste for the Gothic and the 'Chinese', the first a travesty of mediaeval shapes, the second an attempt to suggest the pagodas of an unknown country.

There were dozens of London cabinet-makers, Chippendale's rivals, busy following the current fashions—Ince and Mayhew, William Vile, William Hallet. Chippendale, who made a lasting reputation with his *Director* and whose style is always associated with the designs in it, was as ready as any of them to change from one whim of fashion to another: some of his firm's best cabinet-making was done in the style of Adam, which is totally different from anything in the *Director*.

Robert Adam was an architect who in the 1760s introduced neo-classicism to Britain—a style already current in France. His severe and scholarly work made brilliant use of a study of classical ornament in Italy. It can be seen at Osterley, Syon and Kenwood. Having designed a house, Adam would go on to design the entire inside, down to the last footstool and carpet.

In the latter part of the century the famous names in furniture are George Hepplewhite and Thomas Sheraton. Hepplewhite claimed no original invention in his *Cabinet-maker and Upholsterer's Guide*, 1788. Most of the items illustrated are Adam simplified for the trade.

Sheraton differed from Chippendale and Hepplewhite in having no workshop. He was a first-rate draughtsman with a flair for furniture design. He could also write, as may be seen in *The Cabinet-maker and Upholsterer's Drawing Book*, 1791-6. This volume illustrates the final phase of neo-classicism, a decade or so of painted satinwood and highly ingenious work tables and washstands. By the turn of the century the tapering legs of the neo-classic school were no longer in the height of fashion: Henry Holland, architect and furniture designer to the Prince of Wales, and designer of Brooks Club, had started a demand for furniture in a stronger, simpler classical style.

George I Double Chair c. 1730

A settee, or love seat, of double chair-back form which matched the fashions in ordinary chairs and was popular in the first half of the 18th century. Spurious examples may sometimes be found, made up out of parts of old chairs.

Early Georgian chairs followed the Queen Anne lines: they had cabriole legs, solid vase splats and very often the characteristic curled-over, Queen Anne arms shown in the drawing. But furniture had become heavier and was made important looking with emphatically carved lion masks, paw feet, and shells augmented with husks. The example shown is walnut.

73

William Kent Chair c. 1730

A George I chair in the baroque style of William Kent, who designed furniture for the very rich to harmonise with the architecture of their houses. It is a crimson-and-gold upholstered piece with the Greek key pattern round the seat frame.

Parts of the decoration—certainly the pendent husks on the uprights—are composed of gesso, for which there was a fashion in the early years of the century. Gesso is a paste of chalk and parchment size. It was applied to part-finished woodwork, carved in fine detail (an easier task than with wood) and then gilded.

George II Corner Chair c. 1740

Corner chairs were introduced in early Georgian days. The back, enclosing two of the sides, was about twelve inches high. They were used for reading and writing and some had places for candlesticks. A simple type, sometimes with a high back, was used in barbers' shops and called a shaving chair.

The example is of walnut and has all four legs in cabriole form, ending in whorl feet, splats carved in the fashionable mid-century manner and the anthemion (honeysuckle) motif on the two forward seat rails.

Chippendale Rococo Chair c. 1750

Eighteenth century cabinet-makers borrowed each
other's ideas, and the extent to which Chippendale
and his assistants invented the designs in the *Director* is uncertain. But this chair, closely resembling one of them, is believed to be Chippendale's
personal invention as well as a characteristic product of his workshops. It has the cupid's bow top
rail that he especially favoured and a carved splat
cleverly made to seem part of it. The feet are
French, the whole being in the rococo manner
introduced from France earlier in the century.

Chippendale Chinese and Gothic c. 1760

A carver (with arms for the person carving) and a single chair. Some Chippendale chairs reflected a mid-century society taste for Gothic and 'Chinese' designs, and had trellis work or Gothic arches as filling for the back. Chippendale was very proud of his Chinoiserie designs and claimed credit for them.

In the 1760s cabriole legs went out of fashion and legs became square and straight. The stretchers which had been dropped because they spoiled the cabriole line were now used again, especially for chairs likely to receive hard wear.

Country Chippendale c. 1780

Like other fashionable pieces, the Chippendale chair was in due course in demand in the country. Rural craftsmen had access to pattern books and made simply carved chairs in the styles of London out of oak, elm and beech. Sometimes the proportions were a little uneasy—or at least different from those of the fashionable models.

The well-made chair above is of a kind that would have been found in provincial town houses rather than farmhouses. It serves as pleasantly as a desk chair as for dining.

Country mansions were furnished strictly in the urban manner.

78

Chippendale Upholstered Chair c. 1750

A chair seen in stately homes open to the public, where the respite it invites is denied by a string tied from arm to arm.

Upholstered chairs of the earlier Georgian period usually had plain over-stuffed seats and backs and part-padded arms. Chippendale's *Director* includes examples of several French-inspired armchairs with light and graceful cabriole legs. The acanthus leaf, shown above, was the favoured motif for the knees of legs. It came out well when carved from mahogany.

London Ladder-back c. 1770

The design had been in use for years in the country and was adopted and elaborated by London cabinet-makers, including Chippendale in the 1760s.* The cross rails, pierced and sometimes carved, follow the wavy line of the cresting rail. Legs were usually straight and square: the front ones of the chair drawn show the final phase of the cabriole form. The term ladder back originated in the 19th century. (See page 103).

* Two firms besides Chippendale's to issue influential pattern books were those of Manwaring, and Ince and Mayhew.

Adam Lyre-back c. 1775

The smaller, taper-legged chairs designed by
Robert Adam, the architect and chief exponent of
the neo-classic style, made Chippendale's chairs
seem old-fashioned.

The new type of chair was lower in the back
than had been customary. When there was a
conventional upright splat, it had a lighter feel.
For this member Adam introduced the elegant
lyre shape, with metal rods, which has since been
much used on furniture.

Adam Oval-back c. 1780

This chair represents Adam's later manner: curving, spidery outlines, greater simplicity. The
design was borrowed direct from France.

The oval-backed chair soon won acclaim, and set
a fashion in 'salon' chairs that lasted a quarter of a
century or more. Most subsequent chairs had the
oval slightly raised above the level of the seat. Like
his other furniture, Adam's gilt or satin-wood
chairs are famed for the delicacy of the low-relief
ornament based on Greek and Roman motifs. Even
the embroidered upholstery showed classical detail.

Adam Shield-back c. 1780

If the elbow chair on the previous page may be called spidery, then this one suggests an insect at bay.

The similarity of Adam chairs to contemporary French ones is partly explained by the fact that fashionable France, too, was having a neo-classic movement. The main factor responsible for the change to a delicately classical style was the interest aroused by excavations at Herculaneum and Pompeii. Adam travelled and studied on the Continent for several years.

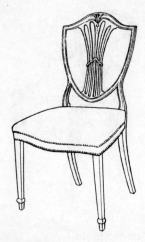

Hepplewhite Shield-back c. 1785

Shield-backs like this are associated with Hepplewhite—and there are plenty in his pattern book, the *Guide*—but the design is believed not to be his invention. The shield would always be raised a few inches above the level of the seat and attractively filled with slender, delicately curved bars. The lines were often broken by such carved motifs as husks, wheatears and rosettes. Canework was used as an alternative filling.

Late 18th Century Camel-back c. 1780

A piece popularly known as Hepplewhite. No chair with a back quite like this appears in Hepplewhite's pattern book, though the waisted splat, resembling a wheatsheaf, and the 'camel' top rail were Hepplewhite devices.

This type of drop-in-seat chair, sometimes with rounded corners at the top, became a favourite with all classes towards the end of the 18th century. The evidence is the large number in various qualities which survive.

Hepplewhite Shield-and-Feathers-back
c. 1790

The three feathers of the Prince of Wales' crest is a device that occurs only once in Hepplewhite's pattern book. But it caught on, and was used again and again in chairs of the Hepplewhite school.

This armchair is of a type that was much in demand at the end of the 18th century. It is painted beech. Were it not for the fine workmanship of the back, it would be an example of a common practice of copying elegant chairs cheaply by means of paint in place of carving and marquetry.

Sheraton Parlour Chair c. 1790

Sheraton liked the term parlour chair, to judge
from his repeated use of it in the *Cabinet-maker and
Upholsterer's Drawing Book.*

Backs with straight lines and square shapes had
been drawn by Hepplewhite, but for Sheraton they
became a speciality. He was critical of Hepplewhite's use of curves—except for arms. His
earlier square backs were filled with vertical
uprights. Sheraton liked plenty of turning. In some
chairs, like that above, even the top rail is turned—
it is fitted between raking and slightly scrolled-
over uprights.

Sheraton Cane-seat c. 1800

In the late 18th century chairs grew ever lighter,
the less expensive variety in beech, painted or gilt,
differing only in detail from those in mahogany or
rosewood. Round front legs with peg-top feet had
ousted square legs by the end of the century and
Sheraton was favouring splats running from side
to side between the uprights.

Reeding was becoming a fashionable form of
decoration; Sheraton pointed out that an odd
number of reeds on a flat surface was easier on the
eye than an even number. The arms of the chair
above have a typically Sheraton S shape.

Country Sheraton c. 1800

The influence of Sheraton, like that of other London furniture designers, affected chair-making in the provinces. The uncompromisingly square back of this country chair would have had the master's approval. Like many country pieces, however, it shows a mixture of influences: the arms, for instance, are treated in the Chippendale manner and screwed to the sides of the seat instead of rising from the front legs.

Hall Chair c. 1780

The hall chair has a history going back to the first half of the 18th century. Describing their use, Sheraton stated that they were to be 'placed in halls for the use of servants or strangers waiting on business'.

They were not meant to be comfortable. The late 18th and early 19th century hall chair almost invariably had a dished wooden seat and a wooden back. A space was left in the back for painting on the family crest.

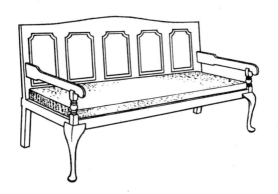

Lancashire Low-back Settle c. 1740

A settee-like development of a type of joiner-made bench furniture which had been in use for centuries in cottage, farmhouse and tavern (the settee, of which there is an example on page 93, is derived from the chair). Earlier settles had high, draught-stopping backs and usually wings instead of arms. Low-backed settles by no means took their place, and plenty of high-backed ones were made in the 19th century.

The piece drawn here is a curious mixture of typical early Georgian oak panelling, cabriole front legs and primitive plank arms which show traces of the Tudor and early Stuart shape.

Bergère c. 1785

A type which was made from the middle of the
century onwards—and usually with sides, back and
seat of canework rather than the light upholstery
shown above. Bergère is the French word for
large armchair (as well as for a shepherdess); it was
rendered by 18th century cabinet-makers 'burjair'
and 'bergier'.

However large, these armchairs differ from
modern upholstered easy chairs in that the wooden
framework (almost always mahogany) dominates
the shape and is visible. Legs, arm supports and
top rail are carefully designed and carved.

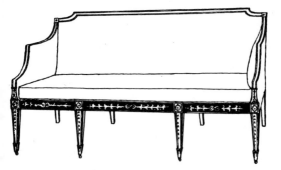

Late 18th Century Settee c. 1790

Like the double chair, the settee proper was an extension of a plain armchair and followed the same trend in design. This one has a back in the Hepplewhite-Sheraton style, and the square tapered legs with spade feet liked by Hepplewhite. It is decorated with gilt on a black ground.

The Georgian sofa, or couch, on the other hand, was a descendant of the day bed and was a more floridly shaped piece. It could be lolled on in a manner that would be impossible with the prim settee.

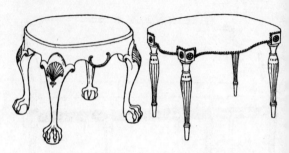

An Early and a Late Georgian Stool
c. 1740 and c. 1775

Throughout the Georgian period stools would be
included in a fashionable set of seating furniture
and dotted about a drawing-room to break the
monotony of numerous identical chairs. These
stools, with either drop-in or upholstered seats,
faithfully reflected current styles for chairs.

The two drawn above illustrate the change that
took place between the reigns of George I and
George III. The first, with its monumental cabriole legs, is typically early Georgian. The second
represents the neo-classic fashion of the Hepplewhite period, in which, among other features, the
seat rails of upholstered furniture were fully
covered by material held down by brass-headed
nails.

Comb-back Windsor c. 1710

There are several varieties of the Windsor chair, but all have one structural feature in common: a solid, saddle-shaped seat which holds the rest in place. The stick components would be turned with a pole lathe where the wood was felled and then driven into the holes bored for them.

The main centre for these comfortable and resilient country chairs was, and is, High Wycombe, Bucks. They are supposed to have been called Windsor in honour of George III who liked some he saw in a cottage while sheltering from heavy rain; but the name appears in auctioneers' catalogues before he came to the throne.

Comb-back Windsor c. 1725

A rather more lively and better proportioned specimen—it is similar to a chair owned by Oliver
Goldsmith. The legs are purposefully turned and
linked by stretchers. The arms, as before, are
formed of one continuous piece of wood.

A Windsor chair is usually found to be made of a
mixture of woods—even five different kinds. Elm
was favoured for the seat and beech for the legs,
but ash, yew, birch and fruitwoods were used freely
for other parts. The country craftsmen did their
work, in fact, with whatever came easiest to hand.

Hoop-back Windsor c. 1750

The practice of bending wood became common towards the middle of the century and the comb cresting bar was overtaken by a hoop-shaped piece of wood that was made to form a framework for the back. The stretcher, too, was given a crinoline shape. The wood was made pliable by steaming and then forced into shape round an iron block.

The example above has two other features which became usual: arms made separately from the back and a couple of diagonal stays to give extra support for the back.

Chippendale-splat Windsor c. 1755

A splat was often introduced and reflected the fashions of the town in an otherwise very traditional article. The splat was never taken up in America where Windsor chairs were made in large numbers (it is recorded that Jefferson sat in one for signing the Declaration of Independence in 1776).

Cabriole legs, as here, were sometimes put on Windsors between 1740 and 1770—another attempt to urbanise an essentially country chair—but they never failed to look incongruous. It is almost impossible to make a satisfactory joint between Windsor seat block and curving legs.

Comb-and-splat Windsor c. 1760

An example of the so-called Chippendale splat being fitted to a double-back Windsor which retains the early form: comb-cresting and only rudimentary turning of unstretchered, stick legs.

Output of Windsor chairs increased in the middle of the 18th century because of demand for them by coffee houses and pleasure gardens; these were spreading on the outskirts of London and other large towns. Old Windsors may still be seen in inns, their legs often shortened by constant wear on stone floors.

Hepplewhite-splat Windsor c. 1780

After the Chippendale splat came the Hepplewhite splat incorporating the Prince of Wales' feathers device. Unlike some of the other 18th century splats, notably the wheel variety on the next page, this one does not seem to have been taken up by 20th century makers of Windsor chairs.

By the 1780s the turning of the legs has an almost modern look, and the ornamental crinoline, or hooped stretcher, has given way to three straight ones.

Wheel-back Windsor c. 1785

The Windsor chair has remained in demand in a
way equalled by no other chair design—and the
wheel device introduced late in the 18th century
has made the most popular splat. It is easy to see
the appeal of these chairs: hardwearing, elegant,
comfortable and cheap to make, they look well in
any non-formal setting.

In the 18th and early 19th centuries Windsors
were often left plain and unpolished, and self-
respecting cottagers would scour them with sand.
Some, however, were painted dark green or black.

Mendlesham Chair, Norfolk Chair c. 1800

These could be called the Windsor chairs of East
Anglia. Technically they are Windsors, since the
seat holds back, arms and legs in position, and
the stickwork involved in making them is that of the
turner rather than the joiner. They remained very
popular till well into the 19th century. The elaborate backs of both kinds were decorated with
small balls. Seats were usually elm and the other
parts fruitwood.

The Mendlesham (Suffolk) chair is sometimes
called a Dan Day after an East Anglian chair-
maker of that name.

Lancashire (or Yorkshire) Ladder-back c. 1785

A country chair differing in construction from the Windsor in that the seat, normally rush-filled, depends on the framework rather than the other way round; back and arms are extensions of the legs. Ladder-backs were introduced in the first half of the 18th century and have always been associated with the northern half of England.

Horizontal slats suggesting the rungs of a ladder had been used from time to time since mediaeval days. Those of the chair drawn are pleasingly formed and arranged. (See page 80.)

Lancashire Spindle-back c. 1785

This chair, with its inset rows of spindles, appears to be a development of the 17th century Carver chair. Like the better kind of ladder-back (its contemporary) on the previous page, it normally had two club feet resting on turned balls, and the part of the front supports immediately below the arms were baluster-turned.

These chairs are especially connected with Lancashire, though they were made elsewhere in the north. Lancashire-made ones tend to have their spindles bunched towards the middle of the back, leaving gaps at each end of the rows.

Child's Lancashire Rocker c. 1800

A replica in miniature of a standard kind of rocking chair used in kitchens, studies and garden-rooms. The fitting of rockers, or bends, to any of the more robust chairs in fashion was introduced towards the end of the 18th century. The one drawn here is made of elm.

Strong little chairs for children have been made since mediaeval times—and not only for those of the rich. In the 18th century every kind of grown-up's chair had its replica in miniature.

Cricket Table c. 1710

Various explanations have been offered for the
name of this country table: the similarity of the
three legs to cricket stumps (although only two
were used in the 18th century), a fancied affinity
with the chirping, jumping cricket of the hearth.

It is now believed to come from the old word
cricket, or cracket, meaning a three-legged stool.
Cricket tables are companionable pieces associated
with the draughty warmth of an open cottage fireplace. Examples with turned legs, as above, are
more rare than those with plain legs.

Mid-18th Century Gate Table c. 1750

A type of mahogany dining or occasional table which had a long run. The finely carved legs with ball and claw feet make this a showy example; usually the legs tapered to pad feet, though they might have a suggestion of the cabriole shape.

This comely and serviceable table—it may be round or oval—is a simplified version of the Stuart gate-leg variety; gates to support rule-jointed flaps swing out on modern hinges from the central frame, whose top, it will be found, is fixed with screws driven in below at an angle.

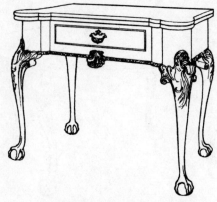

George I Card Table c. 1740

Playing card games for money was one of the pleasures of life in the early part of the 18th century, and some splendid card tables were made. They began to appear in Anne's reign. When opened, the top presented a square of glued-down cloth set in a border of veneer; round, extended corners were dished for money or counters and left room for a candle.

In the walnut example above, with asymmetrical rococo ornament, one leg is hinged to the back framework and swings out to receive the flap. This gate arrangement produced a slightly ungainly effect and the ingenious device seen on the next page gained some favour.

Concertina Card Table c. 1745

The drawing shows the improvement to card tables that came in about 1730 (and another set of magnificent cabriole legs). The framework was hinged in such a way that the flap was supported by *both* back legs; this made the opened table firmer, and gave it a better appearance since all four sides now looked alike. The concertina was more expensive and did not replace the gate type entirely.

When not being played on, card tables did useful service as side tables. Their width, by the way, seems always to have been about three feet.

109

Eagle Table c. 1730

A baroque variety of console, or bracket, table which typifies the lavish interior decoration enjoyed by the rich in the first half of the 18th century. Console tables, often with marble top, were introduced from France; like side tables, they would be arranged to form a group with a looking glass. Having the support in the form of an eagle with outstretched wings became a fashion.

Console tables embellished in this extravagant way are to be seen in several stately homes open to the public. The eagle is usually gilded pine. The base would be of 'marbled' wood.

110

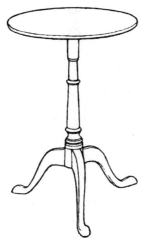

Country Tripod Table c. 1755

Tables with only three legs tended to rest securely on uneven floors in farmhouses and cottages. This is an example (in yew) of the general run of tripod tables which were made in large quantities in the second half of the 18th century. The drawing shows up the basic form of the tripod base, which hardly varied between 1740 and 1780. It consists of inclined cabriole legs dovetailed into the base of the pillar. This is seen to be of simple baluster outline. The feet are the plain pad type.

111

Dumbwaiter c. 1735

The dumbwaiter on tripod base was an English invention of George I's reign. Mahogany had just been introduced; hard and easy to carve, it was found ideal for pieces of this sort which had to be serviceable as well as pretty. The carving of the acanthus leaves on the shaft of the specimen drawn is noticeably crisp.

Dumbwaiters, between four and five feet high, would be put round the dining table at dessert time. The tiers revolved and were within easy reach of the seated diner. The shaft and tripod design gave way to more elaborate forms at the end of the century, some having four legs.

Mid-Georgian Tea Table c. 1750

Tea-drinking became a craze in the middle of the 18th century—for both sexes—and helped slightly to improve manners by reducing the time spent drinking wine after dinner. The taking of tea often went on in a room set aside for the purpose, where each person would have his own table.

A peculiarity of tripod tea tables, sometimes called china tables, is either a gallery or pie-crusting round the top to prevent china falling off. The example above has a spirally shaped shaft and acanthus leaves on the legs.

Neo-classic Tripod Table c. 1790

Tripod tables were often hinged and were made with a variety of tripod bases. In the neo-classic period, following 1780, solid tops gradually gave way to inlaid or painted tops, and cabriole-shaped claws took on the more refined and somehow less satisfactory convex shape seen above. The claws rested on minute pointed feet.

In the 18th century claw table was a more usual term than tripod table.

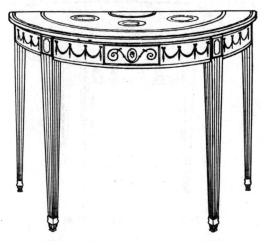

Neo-classic Pier Table c. 1785

A pier table is a side table which will stand conveniently against a pier between Georgian windows. Usually such pieces had an ornamental looking-glass, a pier glass, fixed above them to form a single decorative unit.

The drawing is of a satinwood and marquetry pier table in a characteristic neo-classic style. The design on the top shows it to be one of a pair which can be placed together to form a round central table.

Pembroke Table c. 1790

A type first made in the 1760s but associated especially with Sheraton, who considered it suitable for 'a gentleman or lady to breakfast on'; the design is in fact similar to the breakfast tables illustrated by Chippendale. The two flaps, usually with rounded corners, rested on hinged fly brackets. A drawer would be fitted at one end of the central part and a sham drawer-front at the other end.

There was a considerable output of light, drawered tables on turned or taper legs in the late 18th century. The Pembroke was often made a vehicle for marquetry work. The example drawn is of mahogany inlaid with tulipwood.

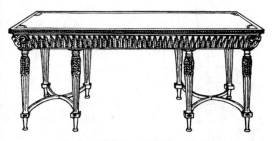

Neo-classic Side Table c. 1775

Since the Restoration the ornamental side table had taken the place in well-to-do dining-rooms of the earlier court cupboard. The dresser, decendant of the court cupboard, was a piece designed for farm-houses and servants' halls.

Intended for display and for serving, side tables were made in numerous designs. For about a quarter of a century from 1735 they carried a hand-some marble or slate slab. Marble tops were to some extent out of favour by Adam's neo-classic period, and the large mahogany table drawn here has an inlaid top; its slender fluted legs and husk ornament carved in low relief are typical of the neo-classic style.

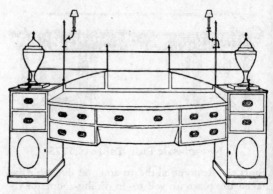

Sideboard with Pedestals c. 1785

The piece of furniture now thought of as a sideboard, something with drawers and cupboards, was developed by Robert Adam. The earliest sort was a group consisting of side table and two separate pedestal cupboards at either end. In due course the three units were made as one, as seen above.

One pedestal was lined with tin and used as a plate-warmer; the other often had a little cupboard at the back for a chamber pot. The urns might be fitted as knife cases, or they would hold water for minor washing-up jobs to be done by the butler.

Bow-front Sideboard c. 1790

Late in the 1780s and 1790s the sideboard in its 'modern' shape appeared—though one of the two end cupboards, taking the place of pedestals, might still house a chamber pot. The drawing shows an unusually small, bow-fronted sideboard in the Hepplewhite-Sheraton style; it is made of mahogany inlaid with box and satinwood. Six legs, four in the front and two at the back, was a usual number at the time. The bay in the middle left room for a wine cooler. A brass rail for supporting plates would be fitted only to bigger sideboards.

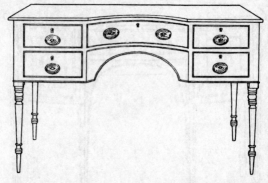

Sideboard with Concave Front c. 1790

Sideboards had become extremely popular by the end of the century, and they were made with serpentine and other kinds of curved fronts. Sheraton wrote of the type drawn here: '... if the sideboard be near the entering door of the dining room, the hollow front will sometimes secure the butler from the jostles of the other servants.'

The example has the rounded legs which were now often used as an alternative to straight tapering ones.

Mid-18th Century (Lancashire) Dresser
c. 1745

A splendid oak example with well-proportioned cornice, and panels architecturally moulded and splayed. Eighteenth century dressers were more commodious than the Stuart kind. The numerous solid drawers, the cupboards (variously placed) and the shelves for china and pewter encouraged domestic order in farmhouse kitchens and kitchen-living-rooms. Dressers were made with a simple graciousness worthy of the dominating position they demanded, yet they remained homely, not attempting the lines of the dining-room sideboard.

121

Early Georgian Bookcase c. 1730

The freestanding bookcase above is in William Kent's style and demonstrates an extreme form of the architectural manner favoured for big houses in the early Georgian period. It is made of grained pine; but stonework rather than cabinet-making is suggested by its monumental, baroque character. Such pieces were considered by Horace Walpole 'immeasurably ponderous'.

Kent was one of the first architects and decorative designers to insist on furniture being an essential part of an architect's work on a house.

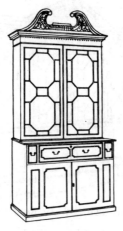

Chippendale Bookcase c. 1750

Bookcases became slightly less architectural in character towards the middle of the century. The trend is shown by those illustrated in Thomas Chippendale's famous *Gentleman's and Cabinet-maker's Director* published in 1754.

Chippendale liked the swan-necked pediment seen on the example above. The drawer front of the cupboard section is hinged to fall flat for writing. The glazing bars were now made from hard Spanish mahogany and were thinner.

Neo-classic Break-front Bookcase c. 1780

A large bookcase with a central section that pro-
trudes. Here Adam-style classical ornament runs
beneath the cornice, while above it rises a broken
pediment being used, as was intended, to accommodate a bust.

All 18th century bookcases had an architectural
look, but the neo-classical movement of the last
thirty years of the century brought renewed emphasis on architectural discipline to their design.
The results were less ponderous than in the Kent
era. The upper classes read more now, and plenty
of big bookcases of this sort were made for their
houses. Some cabinet-makers almost specialised
in them.

124

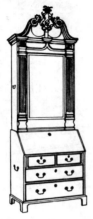

George I Bureau Cabinet c. 1725

A walnut, slanting-front bureau of Queen Anne style, made imposing by the grandeur of the cabinet fitted on top of it. The swan-necked pediment with gilded ornament and the fluted pilasters flanking the door were typical of the architectural style of the early Georgian period. The heavy mirror plate was shortly to be replaced by panelling or panes of clear glass.

Tall pieces of this sort would often stand against the pier between two windows, though they were not necessarily designed for the purpose.

Mid-18th Century Bureau Bookcase c. 1760

The drawing shows a piece of good proportions and workmanship made in a simplified version of the Chippendale style. The type, with more or less simply moulded cornices, continued to be turned out well into the 19th century. An arrangement of thirteen panes of glass for each door is characteristic.

'Desk and bookcase' was the sensible term in use in the 18th century. Examples which appear in Chippendale's *Director* have masses of rococo carving (especially in the gadroon pattern), broken pediments, ogee feet and finely chased handles.

Hepplewhite Secretaire Bookcase c. 1785

From about 1740, or earlier, desks were beginning to be made with the fittings and writing place concealed in a kind of top drawer and given the name of secretary or secretaire.

This secretaire bookcase with serpentine apron-piece connecting bracket feet—a typical Hepplewhite feature—looks exactly like a chest of drawers when shut together. What appears to be the top drawer comes out a few inches, whereupon its front, which is hinged at the bottom, swings down to provide a writing flap. It is held, as shown, by a pair of quadrant stays.

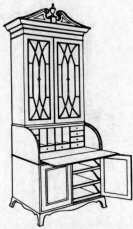

Sheraton Cylinder-front Bureau Bookcase
c. 1795

The rigid cylinder-front was another late 18th century alternative to the oblique flap—and one much favoured by Sheraton. It was made of segments of wood glued together and veneered. When lifted it travels up and over in grooves to take up a position behind the pigeon holes. A slide pulls out to extend the writing surface.

Sheraton legs were often outward-curving and slender. For his more fashionable pieces he followed the swan-necked pediment tradition and, like Hepplewhite, made patterns with the glazing bars.

Tambour-front Bureau c. 1795

The tambour-front, or roll-top, bureau was a variant of the cylinder-front. Tambour is a cabinet-making term for a flexible shutter consisting of thin strips of pine or mahogany, often reeded, which are glued to a backing of canvas. It rests within grooves and can be moved up or down at a touch. An ingenious and pleasing invention of the period, the tambour shutter was often used on 'night tables' and pot cupboads.

Kneehole Writing Table c. 1765

Originally a dressing table design. Chippendale, in the third edition of the *Director*, gives eleven examples, all intended for dressing at. Small compartments and a rising mirror would be found either on pulling out the long drawer or on lifting up the top (when, of course, the drawer-front would be a dummy).

No doubt these dressing tables were often used for writing. At any rate they soon came to be made without toilet fittings. The drawing shows a typical mid-century model: central cupboard, writing slide, plain bracket feet, rococo mounts to the handles.

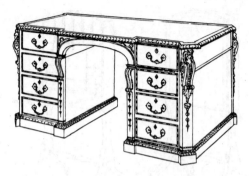

Library Table or Pedestal Desk c. 1765

Much enlarged versions of kneehole writing tables,
minus central cupboard and—usually—top drawer,
were made for libraries, where they stood in the
middle of the room. The idea was hardly new,
since Pepys had an oak pedestal desk of this kind
in the previous century (it is now at Magdalene
College, Cambridge).

A pedestal desk like the rococo example drawn
is big enough for two people to sit facing each
other. Often these desks were made in two parts—
to stand back to back or separately against the wall.

Lady's Writing Fire Screen c. 1790

An easy-to-move luxury article which enabled the writer of letters to sit before the fire and yet have her face shielded from its direct rays. The name is contemporary. The usual size of the top part was twenty inches wide by three inches deep. A slightly more robust model was made for men.

The writing fire screen was introduced by Thomas Shearer, a cabinet-maker who had a hand in compiling a book of great interest to furniture historians, *The Cabinet-makers' London Book of Prices*.

132

Carlton House Table c. 1795

With its tapering, unimpeded legs this has more the feeling of a writing table than a desk. A superstructure of small drawers and cupboards hedges in the top, leaving only a small writing space. Intended for women's use, the type was sometimes called 'a Lady's Drawing and Writing Table'.

It was named Carlton House (by the firm Gillows of Lancaster) after the residence of the Prince of Wales, for whom the original design was prepared.

Flap-and-Tambour Desk c. 1795

Numerous little writing tables, in mahogany or satinwood, were produced in the late 18th and early 19th centuries. The workmanship was such that in spite of a delicate appearance they could be very strong.

The piece drawn is of inlaid mahogany with fluted, tapering legs. It is made with great precision: as the drawer is pulled out, so the tambour cover recedes. The flap opens to reveal a writing slope and drawers.

Commode c. 1770

An ornate chest of drawers in the French taste intended for the drawing-room rather than the bed-room. The example drawn is restrained as com-modes went, but has the characteristic basic features: serpentine front, doors enclosing the drawers and French legs. It is an oak piece embel-lished with satinwood veneer and marquetry of various woods, including cross-banded borders of harewood. The front corners are finished with cast mounts of gilt brass.

The word commode was not used for a night chair till the 19th century.

Hanging Corner Cupboard c. 1740

Cupboards to be hung in corners seem to have
originated in the last years of the 17th century.
They were made throughout the 18th and early
19th centuries, in oak or mahogany. They were
mainly cottage pieces designed to save space,
though plenty of ornamental examples are to be
seen which obviously were not intended for small
dwellings. Fronts were usually flat, with a panel
to the door. As any possessor of a corner cupboard
knows, the outside promises more useful room
inside than there actually is.

136

George I Chest of Drawers on Stand c. 1720

Here is a very handsome example of the chest-on-drawered-stand arrangement, the forming of which had become a practice late in the previous century. Quarter columns in the Corinthian style flank the chest; matched walnut veneers, cross-banded for borders, cover front and sides of the oak carcase.

Unstretchered George I cabriole legs needed to be strong and well-fitted for a piece of this size, and somehow those shown here give the impression that they are: a tenseness about the eagle-claw feet suggests ability to carry weight.

Beading was now applied to the edges of drawers instead of to the rails between them.

Tallboy c. 1755

The tallboy, or chest on chest, first appeared early in the 18th century. After about 1725 it began to take the place of the chest on stand, the legs of which had proved vulnerable. The upper chest, often bevelled at the corners to offset the massive effect, had a top row of two or three small drawers which could be reached only by standing on a chair. The inconvenience of this caused the tallboy to go out of fashion towards the end of the century.

The solid mahogany specimen drawn here has typical mid-century features: stuck-on 'Chinese' fretwork, a dentil pattern in the cornice moulding, elaborate bracket feet and rococo handles.

Mid-18th Century Chest of Drawers c. 1760

The typical mid-century chest of drawers—mahogany with oak drawer-linings—remained plainly rectangular, but it had richly double-curved (ogee) feet and ornate rococo handles. When mahogany was used as a veneer the carcase would be of red deal and often left plain at the sides. Many chests were made smaller now, with three long drawers and two short.

The cock bead, or semi-circular moulding, round the drawer edges continued standard practice for the rest of the century.

Hepplewhite Chest of Drawers c. 1785

Ordinary bedroom furniture of the last twenty years of the 18th century was influenced more by Hepplewhite than Sheraton. The latter went in for complex and elaborate designs. Hepplewhite chests of drawers were either serpentine-fronted or, as here, bow-fronted. They had outward-turning feet ('French' style) which were attached directly to the chest without protruding plinth; curving apron-pieces ran between the feet.

When mahogany was used as a veneer it was generally applied to a deal carcase. The better pieces had oak drawer-linings.

Fitted Dressing Table c. 1750

The hinged top of this piece offered the advantage of a built-in looking glass attached in a frame as shown. The disadvantage, compared with the type with drawer, is that before opening, anything placed on the top must be removed.

The family resemblance to the Queen Anne dressing table (page 68) is especially obvious in the treatment of the cabriole legs. Drawerless varieties, disclosing numerous partitions for cosmetics and articles of the toilet, remained in vogue throughout the Georgian period.

**Box Toilet (or Dressing) Glasses c. 1710
and 1795**

The small swing mirror held between posts was a
beginning-of-the-century innovation. Mounted on
a box equipped with an arrangement of miniature
drawers, it was more interesting than the glass on
strut supports which was also made.

The earlier mirrors were upright rectangles with
an arched heading; the walnut-veneered drawers
below would have concave fronts. Then came
oval and shield shapes—often in satinwood. At the
end of the century the usual shape became a
rectangle set lengthwise between turned posts.
The cheval glass, made concurrently, was a bigger
piece with trestle, or horse, support and sometimes
a pulley device for moving the glass.

Bureau Dressing Table c. 1730

A dressing table of two-drawer, bureau form. Basically this is the small box toilet glass shown on the previous page; but here it is enlarged and given long cabriole legs to make it an independent piece of furniture instead of an article to be put on a dressing table or chest of drawers. Equally suitable of course, for writing at, the bureau dressing table was first introduced early in the century.

George I Clothes Press c. 1730

For most of the 18th century clothes press was the term for what would now be called a wardrobe —despite the extremely ample provision of drawers below. Construction in two parts, with moulding to hide the join, was usual. Clothes were laid flat rather than hung and plenty of sliding shelves were provided. The arched pigeon holes of this oak example suggest places for storing articles other than clothes.

The term wardrobe, which to Chaucer meant a privy, did not come to be used in the modern sense until the 1770s.

Hepplewhite Wardrobe c. 1790

In Hepplewhite's *Guide*, 1788, the term wardrobe is found being used for the piece of bedroom furniture that had long been known as a clothes press. Several varieties were illustrated. Hepplewhite regarded the wardrobe as 'an article of considerable consequence', and recommended door panels of figured mahogany edged by satinwood inlays. The typical wardrobe of the last decades of the century, basically of pine, was a simple two-part structure of the kind drawn; though the outward-curving 'French' feet, linked by a serpentine curve, were less usual than simple brackets. Shelves were still considered more useful than hanging space.

K   145

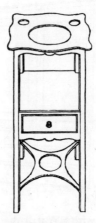

Hepplewhite Washstand c. 1785

Bedroom washstands began to appear in the 1750s. The drawing shows a pretty enough mahogany stand with a hole in the top just big enough to take the minute wash-basin found adequate in Georgian times. Halfway down, the legs are framed-in for a drawer, and below that there is a receptacle for a jug. This was a common type of wash, or basin, stand and large numbers have survived. Some may be seen today doing service as stands for a telephone and telephone books.

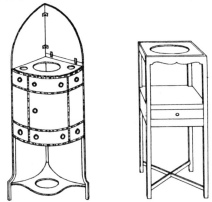

Sheraton Washstands c. 1790

Two of Sheraton's simpler designs for basin stands. Sheraton was particularly good at devising three-legged corner models. The example on the left has two top flaps intended to protect the wall from splashes when raised, and to conceal the basin when lowered. It contains a cupboard and a drawer below it. What appear to be three upper drawers are dummies: sham drawers of this sort are often found on late 18th century bedroom furniture.

147

Sheraton Washstand with Cistern c. 1795

The drawer above the cupboard of this piece had
to be opened with caution. It had the dirty water
from the basin emptied into it, having been lined
with lead for the purpose. Another hazard, as
Sheraton explained in the *Drawing Book*, was that
it would not pull out fully until the basin was
removed.

Above the basin is a small cupboard containing
a supply of water in a cistern and a tap. Sheraton
designed other more complicated wash-hand
pieces; in some of them sham drawer fronts concealed a pull-out bidet.

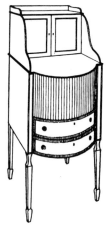

Sheraton Pot Cupboard c. 1795

A cupboard for a chamber pot—and quite elegant with its tapered legs and satinwood finish. Sheraton liked such pieces to be 'in a style a little elevated above their use'. The main cupboard is enclosed by a tambour door—a flexible shutter running in grooves. Sheraton explained that the small upper cupboard was 'intended to keep medicines to be taken in the night, or to hold other little articles which servants are not permitted to overlook'.

The pot cupboard, according to Hepplewhite, was 'an article much used in bed-chambers, counting houses, offices, etc.'

149

Fourposter c. 1740

The lofty fourposters of the big houses became
lighter in construction when mahogany began to
take the place of walnut in the 1730s. The back
posts were allowed to merge with a carved board.
The front ones were made as handsomely as pos-
sible. They were turned and carved above mattress
level and rested on brief cabriole legs embellished
with claw-and-ball feet. Cornices, which had pre-
viously been of deal and covered in fabric, were
now   unveiled   structures   of   carved   wood.
Gadrooning was a favourite ornament. Later in
the century cornices were sometimes made in a
serpentine shape, and square pedestals replaced
cabriole legs.

REGENCY PERIOD
1800—1830

PRINCE George was Regent from 1811 to 1820. 'Regency', however, has become a convenient label for the first thirty years of the 19th century. The main furniture styles of this period are the most emphatically classical that England has known.

Adam and his followers in the neo-classic school had used antiquities mainly as a source of inspiration for ornament. Now it became the fashion to copy the actual furniture of classical times, examples of which were being dug up at Pompeii and elsewhere; and cabinet-makers turned out Greco-Roman chairs, tripods and couches. There was even a vogue for mahogany versions of Egyptian stone furniture. For things without precedent in antiquity, like bookcases, an attempt was made to imagine the designs a Greek or a Roman would have thought of.

The new taste was largely inspired by the heavy Empire style of Napoleonic France: Regency furniture is still sometimes known as 'English Empire'. Thomas Hope, a traveller and amateur architect, spread the archaeological manner in England with a book called *Household Furniture and Interior Decoration*, published in 1807. It

A Regency Interior c. 1820

152

contained a striking collection of reproduced and adapted items of classical furniture. Mostly their lines were bare and simple, but a few sported fantastic human and animal supports.

It was these which seemed to interest George Smith, a professional cabinet-maker, whose *Collection of Designs*, 1808, drew the attention of the trade to numerous wild inventions. The book contained 158 plates in colour, all 'studied from the best antique examples'.

But the Georgian tradition of cabinet-making remained, and the general run of furniture produced by the new movement continued to be handsome in a restrained way, if sometimes clumsy. By comparison much of the contemporary French furniture was rather harsh and strident. In France, however, Empire had become an ideological style reflecting a newly inspired nation's sympathy with the triumphs of Athens and Rome. It spread to uniforms and women's dresses.

Of the various styles adopted in the period— these include a revival of the 'Chinese' japanned manner—it was the severe style of ancient Greece, copied from vase paintings, which predominated. Interest in Greece was furthered by the purchase in 1816 of the Parthenon sculptures, and up to about 1830 new furniture was proudly described as being in the 'modern, Grecian style'. 'An ordinary chair in the most ordinary parlour,' wrote Sir Walter Scott in 1828, 'has now something of an antique cast, something of the Greek massiveness ... that of twenty or thirty years since was mounted on four tapering and tittering legs resembling four tobacco-pipes.'

The most noticeable feature of Regency furniture is the addition of brass to the wood. This became a specialised craft in London. Brass inlay was longer-lasting than marquetry, and made an excellent finish. Its popularity led to a rich man's revival of the Restoration fashion for French Boulle decoration—the inlaying of ebony and tortoise-shell with various metals. Other characteristics are reeding, sabre legs and a plentiful use of rosewood. The Regency phase continued into the latter part of William IV's reign, but by then a growing emphasis on solidity was leading to the ugly lines and ill-placed decoration which marred much of the furniture that lay ahead.

Thomas Hope X-back c. 1810

Based on the designs of ancient Greece, the typical Regency chair (probably rosewood) had front and back legs that curved boldly outwards. These are usually called sabre legs. The 'Grecian' chair drawn here, with X-shaped back-filling and broad, concave top rail riding over the uprights, is one of several which closely resembles the ancient Greek chair, the klismos, seen in vase paintings. A chair design with many offspring, it was recommended by Thomas Hope, a connoisseur of architecture and furniture whose book of designs greatly influenced Regency taste.

**Rope-back, or Trafalgar, Dining Chair
c. 1815**

Grecian chairs with a smaller top rail that was fitted within scrolled-over uprights became even more popular than the sort on the previous page—and they are much reproduced today. The centre bar of the back, usually slightly concave, often took the nautical rope-twist form (suggested by sea battles) shown in the loose-seated example above. Another device was a slat inlaid with brass.

A peculiarity of these clean-lined chairs is that their sides—legs, seat frame and back upright—are entirely flush. Rest one on its side, and it will be found to touch the floor at all points.

Regency Carver's Chair c. 1810

For armchairs, a favourite arm design was an S-shape in which the turned arm-support was done away with. Instead the arms curved down into a semi-circle in such a way that the lower part of the curve could be fixed to the seat frame. These arms could certainly be very handsome, but the unavoidable cross grain at the front of the curve was a structural weakness. The chair drawn has a cane seat beneath its squab cushion. The top rail sports a brass handle for moving the chair as well as honeysuckle decoration of brass inlay. 'Carver's' refers, of course, to its use by the person carving at table.

Library Chair with Steps c. 1805

Steps of some sort were indispensable for reaching the upper shelves in tall libraries; the folding kind was preferred. The drawing shows steps which are assembled by simply pulling forwards and down the back of the comfortable-looking elbow-chair on the left. Since the mid-Georgian period, steps had also been ingeniously fitted into stools and tables. Some incorporated a writing shelf at the summit, enabling the user to make notes without coming down.

George Smith Armchair c. 1805

An 'Egyptian' chair in the manner of George
Smith, cabinet-maker and author of a trade book
of furniture designs. His manner here is that of the
contemporary Empire style of France. There was
a brief ancient Egyptian vogue in England during
the first few years of the 19th century, and chairs
with front legs resembling the legs of an animal
would incorporate brass sphinxes, as here, and
griffins. The sphinx is a winged monster of
Thebes with a girl's head, and the griffin an eagle
with the body of a lion.

159

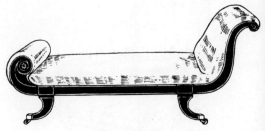

Grecian Couch c. 1805

A usual part of the equipment of the well-to-do Regency interior—and more comfortable than any previous day bed. Very often there was a short arm-rest at the S-shaped end. Instead of outward curving legs, some couches had them turned in the form of tops. The example here is painted and gilt and has brass patera ornaments.

Couch and sofa temporarily ousted the less patrician settee (derived from an armchair) which now tended to serve as hall furniture.

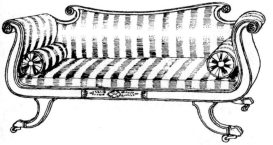

Gilt and Painted Sofa c. 1810

David's painting of Madame de Recamier, the French social leader, pensive on a Grecian couch helped to put all types of Regency sofas high in the esteem of the women of the period. The flowing shapes were meant to recall not only the designs of antiquity but also its manners and customs.

It will be noted in the example that the bold scrolling of the ends—which make a continuous line with the seat rail—is echoed in the shape of the back. Bolster cushions were the normal accompaniment of such sofas.

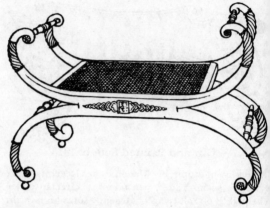

X-frame Music Stool c. 1805

An easily moved stool, often painted, which served as well at the dressing table as at the harpsichord, spinet or piano. Stools were plentiful in Regency interiors and the X-frame, with its classical connections, was the favoured shape. Many seats for window recesses were of X-construction, too, though they would be upholstered rather than caned like this music stool.

162

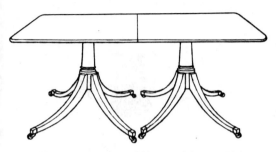

Pillar-and-Claw Dining Table c. 1805

As in the 18th century, dining tables were supplied
in units which could be joined together to give the
required size for a dinner party—twenty-four
inches of space per diner was the accepted allow-
ance.

From about 1800 the customary support for
each section of a fashionable table was a single
pillar with four splayed legs, or claws, ending in
brass toes and castors. Diners certainly had more
room for their knees by this arrangement, though
less for their feet because of conflict with the claws.

George Smith Dining Table c. 1810

Wide use of the pillar-and-claw support inspired designers to take out patents for tables calculated to give diners freedom for their feet as well as their knees. In 1808 George Smith put forward the circular dining table shown above, its fluted pedestal mounted on three perfectly flat claws.

Round tops became very fashionable; it was found that the absence of ends avoided invidious distinctions in the matter of who was to sit where.

As dining tables were covered with a white cloth for meals, their tops commonly did not receive the elaborate decoration given to side tables.

Thomas Hope Monopodium c. 1815

The monopodium illustrates the Regency taste for Egyptian shapes; a massive three-sided base on claw feet, it forms a support that would hold up a house, let alone a marble slab. The small table here (about three feet across) was made from a design by the Regency antiquary, Thomas Hope, and shows strong French influence. It foreshadows, in its ponderousness, something of the heavily ornamental manner of much Victorian furniture.

Drum Table c. 1805

All kinds of round-topped table became popular at the beginning of the 19th century. The drum, or capstan, table on pedestal and claws drawn here is of a type first introduced in the second half of the 18th century. It is mahogany and has twelve drawers.

Some were made with a central well for money and had the encircling drawers alphabetically labelled: these are now generally known as rent tables. A disadvantage with the drum table was that uneven filling of the drawers was inclined to make the top waggle.

Regency Card Table c. 1810

The highly polished rectangular top opens out on brackets to form a perfect square covered with green cloth. In its shut form, the table would be used to hold tea-time things; also to stand against a wall and there 'take upon itself the dignity of a little tidiness'—as Fanny Burney in 1801 wrote of little tables so placed.

The elaborate supporting structure with lion-paw brass feet, the other metal mounts, and the inlaid stringing lines on the frieze stamp this rose-wood piece as unmistakably Regency.

Sheraton Sofa Table c. 1800

A development of the Pembroke table*, and made popular by Sheraton, the sofa table was of a convenient length and height to stand beside a sofa, where a lady would use it for reading, writing and drawing.

It would be about five feet long, with the short flaps put up. There were normally two shallow drawers matched by dummy drawer fronts on the opposite side. Occasionally a rising desk with small drawers was built into the top.

* This continued in favour, especially as a tea table.

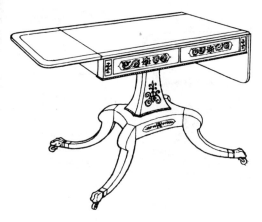

Pedestal Sofa Table c. 1815

The form of the sofa table that came with the fashion for shapes reminiscent of classical times. Its top part rests on a pedestal support which is mounted on a platform with four rugged brass-ended claws. The legs of the claws are dovetailed to the platform.

The table drawn is of very high quality: its Greek-influenced decorations in brass are set in a ground of amboyna and kingwood veneer.

Dumbwaiters c. 1805 and 1820

The examples illustrate the move away from the
tripod base to the more solid arrangement of platform and four claws that became a familiar device
for tables. Dumbwaiters, whose tiers revolved, remained in favour for dessert-time use throughout
the Regency period. They enabled the company to
talk freely without servants present. The example
on the left is perhaps unusual in having the top
tier held rigid by brass supports instead of movable
on an extension of the column below.

Regency Side Table c. 1810

The side table went on being made and often had
a top of solid marble. Basically, it was the 18th
century Adam-style sideboard table given the Regency look: this might involve lion supports and
motifs based on mythical Egyptian creatures.

The small table drawn—mahogany with marble
top—is comparatively restrained, but the prominent carved paws, with plinths to go beneath,
and the choice of applied brass motifs make it an
article in the height of fashion. The brass gallery
is a typical late 18th century and Regency feature.

171

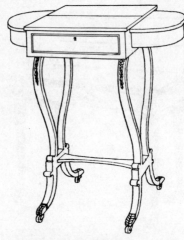

Regency Work Table c. 1805

Small tables abounded in Regency drawing-rooms and boudoirs, and none were in more constant use, one gathers, than the ladies' work tables. The usual provision was a lifting top disclosing compartments and, below, a pleated silk pouch for needlework. The example here (with pouch missing) has a shallow fitted drawer and two semi-circular containers with hinged lids.

Since the late 18th century numerous versions of the lady's work table had been appearing on the market.

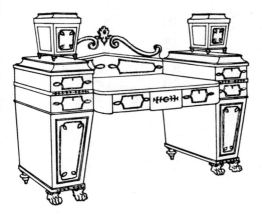

Pedestal Sideboard c. 1820

The 18th century dining-room arrangement of side table flanked by cellaret pedestals returned to fashion in the Regency; but before long the three units were assembled into one massive piece of furniture, a type of sideboard that continued into the 19th century.

A tapering shape for both the bottle-holding pedestals and the knife boxes on top of them became customary after about 1820. Brass rails behind the table part gave way to a carved back piece, a feature which was to assume elaborate proportions in Victorian times. The example drawn is of rosewood, richly inlaid with brass.

Chiffonier c. 1810

A low cabinet with display shelves which became very popular for drawing-rooms and libraries. It largely took the place of the late 18th century commode, a piece too much curved and decorated to suit the Regency taste for plainer surfaces. The name comes from the French *chiffonière*, a type of small chest of drawers on legs.

The list of brass fittings for giving furniture an elegantly finished look now included the wire lattice seen on the door of the cupboard above. This brasswork, usually backed by a silk curtain, is echoed by four brass rods embellishing the upper stage.

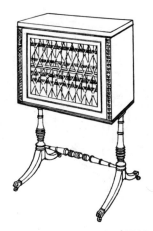

Bookcase on Stand c. 1810

This type of small bookcase with its trellis of brass wire is very much a Regency innovation; it usefully supplemented the great two-stage bookcases which continued to be made. Another portable piece introduced had a revolving container for the books.

The bookcase drawn is of rosewood. There was an idea at this time that rosewood was appropriate for the drawing-room and that mahogany went best in the dining-room and the library.

175

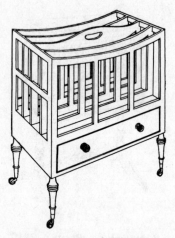

Canterbury c. 1810

A castored stand for sheet music which could be pushed beneath the keyboard of a piano when not in use.

The word canterbury was also used for a stand on castors to hold cutlery and plates, a forerunner of today's indoor trolley. Sheraton in the *Cabinet Directory*, 1803, suggested that the name was the result of an Archbishop of Canterbury being the first person to order such pieces.

Teapoy c. 1825

Ever since taking tea became fashionable in the early 18th century, the lady of the house liked to have charge of the raw materials; they were kept in a tea-chest standing loose on a small tripod table. The ornamental teapoy (the word is of Hindu origin) was an early 19th century development; it would be fitted with three or four canisters and a couple of mixing bowls.

The specimen above is in rosewood. The over-abundant brass-inlay work illustrates a post-1820 tendency for decoration to become involved and fussy.

M   177

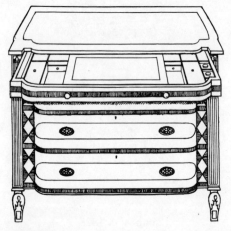

Early Regency Chest of Drawers c. 1805

Modifications to the chest of drawers in the Regency gave it a certain grandeur. The type above, often of satinwood, was inspired by a Sheraton design. The half-columns at the front angles were to become increasingly prominent and ornamental. After 1810 spiral carving would take the place of the reeding shown above, and stylised lion feet that of the turned supports. Bow fronts remained popular throughout the period.

VICTORIAN PERIOD
1830—1901

THE needs of a rapidly swelling middle class caused an enormous increase in furniture production in the second quarter of the 19th century. Machines were used for certain jobs, including much of the carved decoration, but there was no mass production by machinery yet; that came later in the century. The extra output was achieved by battalions of woodworkers. Like the servants for dusting their products, these were easy to find in an England whose population of eight and half million in 1800 doubled itself in fifty years.

By 1835 the clean Grecian lines of the Regency were out of favour except for male rooms. As for Georgian furniture, it was put in attics or given to the poor. Everyone wanted furniture which was graver, more imposing; it had to have plenty of curves, flamboyant ornament and glossy rounded corners—and the more of it in each room the better. Mahogany and rosewood were the favourite woods; and oak became popular again for its weight and Britishness.

Although most Victorian furniture is cumbrous, its debased rococo carving apparently squeezed from a tube, some of the small chairs and stands and articles in papier mâché are today once more

A Victorian Interior c. 1870

finding admirers. Whatever one may say of the great easy chairs and sofas, they are very comfortable. Upholstery and considerations of comfort were now for the first time being allowed to determine the shape of seat furniture.

The most popular styles were the so-called Louis XIV, the Gothic and the Elizabethan. Mixtures of all three were to be seen in many of the grandiose (and not entirely representative) specimens on show at the Great Exhibition of 1851. It was the Gothic style, considered romantic, which had the most lasting effect: A. W. N. Pugin, one of the few early Victorian architects to design furniture, concentrated exclusively on Gothic principles.

The quality of ordinary domestic furniture declined badly after about 1850, a demand for ostentation at a small price leading to poor workmanship, masked by veneer and coarse ornament. A number of designers who tried to introduce tighter, more rational furniture had an effect on public taste, however, and in the sixties the early Victorian manner began to give way to what became known as Art Furniture. Fussy or downright ugly it may be, but in general it was at least better made.

'The backs of sideboards are curved in the most senseless and extravagant manner,' wrote the architect Charles Eastlake in 1868. His book, *Hints on Household Taste*, gives a good idea of the kind of furniture the late Victorians came to like. The emphasis now was on aggressively straight lines, solid wood that was often stained black or dark green, and a sparing use of upholstery; painted patterns replaced carving as an acceptable form of decoration. A variety of old English and Continental styles was adopted and there was a fashion, in the seventies and eighties, for Anglo-Japanese fretwork panels and imitation bamboo supports.

Meanwhile, William Morris, the painter, had founded a firm which set out to demonstrate the superiority of furniture made entirely by hand. It produced simple cabinets, with joints exposed to show their honesty, on which Morris and his pre-Raphaelite friends painted scenes from the mediaeval romances; the firm also specialised in cheap country chairs more pleasing to look at than to sit on.

The influence of Morris helped to bring into being the Arts and Crafts Movement of the eighties: under its banner guilds and societies held exhibitions of articles craftsman-made in the English farmhouse style of the 18th century. Their activities paved the way to the brief, close-of-century reign of Art Nouveau. They also served to draw attention to the merits of late 18th century cabinet work banished by the early Victorians. It was rescued; it was reproduced and faked. The practice, so much with us today, of buying secondhand furniture for one's house began at this time, and antique shops were opened.

**Grecian Chair and Early Balloon-back
c. 1830 and 1835**

The chair on the left with the classical yoke rail
was the standard dining chair in 1830. But in the
next few years it was rapidly succeeded in high
fashion by the more rounded-looking chair on the
right.

This one, in fact, is the earliest of the balloon-
backs, an entirely English type which was to have
a long history. The back did not properly resemble
a balloon until the 1840s (see next page) when top
rail and uprights were formed in a continuous
curve and given a 'waist'.

183

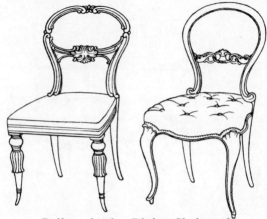

**Balloon-backs: Dining Chair and
Drawing-room Chair c. 1850**

The balloon-back was the standard pattern for up-right chairs until about 1875. Some were still being made in the nineties. The version for the drawing-room was distinguished after 1850 by French-type cabriole legs. Bedroom chairs also took the balloon shape; these were lighter, of course, and often of birch or maple instead of mahogany or rosewood.

Balloon-backs are curiously comfortable, supporting the sitter's shoulders and the small of his back at exactly the points where support is welcome.

Upholstered-back Dining Chair c. 1865

Chairs of this type, with soft backs and scrolled
uprights, came into favour in the 1870s and were
eventually more highly esteemed than the balloon-
backs. However, the design was more expensive
to work up and it cannot be said that they entirely
overtook the earlier variety.

The next fashion in dining-room chairs (in the
eighties and nineties) was for designs inspired by
Chippendale, Hepplewhite and Sheraton.

Upholstered Spoon-back c. 1845

The term spoon-back is used for various small early
Victorian chairs with hollowed backs. This French-
legged, armless kind looks more like a spoon than
most—when seen from the side. From the front,
the back's enclosing band of mahogany (or rosewood), surmounted by a lump of rococo ornament, is seen to be rounded and waisted in the
manner of the popular balloon-backs. Large
numbers of little chairs like this survive and are
easily fitted into modern drawing-rooms. Their
original covering material was usually Berlin
woolwork.

186

Prie-dieu c. 1850

A chair intended for family prayers which often served as a base for the fashionable Berlin wool-work. The padded rail overlapping a very high back made a convenient place for resting the arms.

The prie-dieu (also known by the names vesper and devotional) was a new contribution to chair types by the early Victorians, though the general shape owes something to that of the high-backed chairs of the late 17th century.

Abbotsford Chair c. 1840

A type of chair much in demand in the middle of
the century. It gets its name from the house of
Sir Walter Scott, whose novels encouraged a widespread, romantic preoccupation with 'olden times'.
The style was described as Elizabethan though it
suggested, if anything, the style of the Charles II
era. 'Elizabethan' pieces were illustrated in nearly
every pattern book by the 1840s, and they stayed
popular for over thirty years. Carved ornament of
the sort shown here appeared on a variety of pieces
of furniture.

Papier Mâché Chair c. 1840

The lightness of papier mâché, its smooth moulded appearance when japanned, and the ease with which it could be attractively inlaid with pearl-shell and bits of jewelry led a few early Victorian manufacturers to try their hand at papier mâché furniture as well as just boxes and trays. However, the material proved unsuitable for structural parts: the chair here has a wooden frame and legs.

Papier mâché originated in Paris in the 18th century, when the process consisted of pressing pulped waste paper between dies. The Victorians preferred to paste sheets of paper on moulds.

Early Victorian Easy Chair c. 1850

One of the best proportioned pieces to come out of
the early Victorian period. It is strong and comfortable, the curves of the exposed mahogany
frame are related to one another and the carving
has been used with restraint.

Deeply buttoned chairs of this type were not all
upholstered in leather originally, as is sometimes
supposed; the one shown in *Through the Looking-
Glass*, with Alice curled up in it, has a woollen cover
of some sort. Alice's chair has open space below
the arms and is therefore to be dated rather later
than the example above. Tenniel, in fact, drew it
in the 1870s.

Late Victorian Easy Chair c. 1880

There was a reassuring suggestion of strength and decent comfort about Victorian lounge chairs, as they were often called, especially when the horse-hair padding was tightly enclosed by leather. After about 1875 it was the custom to give such chairs a lighter appearance; the area between arms and seat lost the filling of upholstery.

Chairs like the one drawn remained in use in dining- and smoking-rooms for at least a quarter of a century. Occasionally they were fitted with a small drawer in the front part of the seat for holding a spittoon.

191

Ladies' Easy Chair c. 1850

A chair shape introduced in the Regency period, and in demand for half a century. These low, armless chairs were comfortable as well as elegant; the vast skirts of the Victorian woman spilled over conveniently on either side. The continuous seat and back suggest a forerunner of the modern deck-chair.

Another· mid-century ladies' easy chair was a small, fully upholstered piece with low arms and a high back; it had a deep seat and short turned legs on castors.

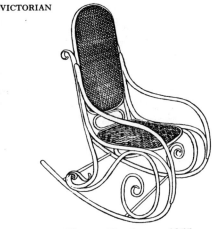

Thonet Rocker c. 1855

The most graceful of the bentwood chairs mass-
produced by the Viennese firm of Thonet. Beech
for the frames was bent into shape by an improved
steaming process.

The bentwood chair that made the firm's reputation was the flimsy, armless kind with a round seat
and a back composed of two hoops, one within
the other; it is a type often seen today in cafés.

Thonet Frères exhibited at the Great Exhibition
of 1851 with such success that they set up an estab-
lishment in London. Their chairs, and those of
their imitators, remained best-sellers for about
sixty years.

Morris Elbow Chair c. 1865

A rush-seated elbow chair of birch, stained black. It was one of the few products of the firm of Morris & Co.—all hand-made in the manner of earlier craftsmen—which could be turned out cheaply. Large quantities were made after 1865, and to this day the chair is being reproduced. The design is based on that of a country chair seen by William Morris, the painter and designer, in Sussex.

Another Morris chair which had a long run, especially in America, was the easy chair with adjustable back, flat wooden arms (padded on top) and loose cushions.

Art Nouveau Chair c. 1895

One of the high-backed chairs by Charles Rennie Mackintosh, a Glasgow architect and a leading Art Nouveau designer. His chairs, usually of dark, stained oak, sometimes had backs that were five feet high. They were designed for a setting predominantly white and black. The 'quaintness' of the style, a word used for it at the time, appealed to certain intellectually inclined people. But the fashion was too extravagant and rootless to last long, and in fact precipitated a burst of interest in period furnishing—'Jacobean', 'Queen Anne', and so on.

Fan-back and Scroll Windsor c. 1830

The simple fan back on the left, with a round and entirely flat seat, is a descendant of a late 18th century Windsor. The design, with variants, has been made ever since.

The variety of scroll Windsor on the right—so named because the uprights begin to scroll over—brought with it something of the Regency form. It was made in quantity throughout the 19th century.

These chairs would usually be beech with elm seats.

Lath-and-baluster Windsor c. 1835

One of the most robust of the Windsor chairs, and a
type commonly used in kitchens, tea gardens and
inns. The bulbous, turned legs and double cross-
stretcher stamp it as typically Victorian.

The example drawn is of beech stained red and
varnished to imitate rosewood. These chairs were
often painted dark green or black. They are usually
known simply as kitchen chairs.

Smoker's Bow c. 1840

A bow-back Windsor, often used in smoking-rooms, which became very popular, too, for public houses, barbers' shops, cottages and offices. It is still seen in such settings; modern versions are made.

The low, semi-circular back of the early Victorian type—as above—would contain either seven or eight spindles. The elegant turnery shown here gave way to a plainer fashioning of the members later in the century.

Drawing-room Sofa c. 1850

The sofa of the 1830s was strictly rectangular in plan with upright arms—as it often is today—but gradually a more flowing and 'French' style was developed until sofas resembled the one drawn here. This mid-century example shows the influence of Louis XIV baroque scrolls and carved cresting.

Deep buttoning, a fashion which began in the early thirties, emphasizes the curves and softness of the upholstery; plenty of attention is given to the exposed parts of the framework.

199

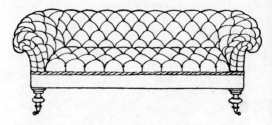

Chesterfield c. 1885

In the latter part of the period the framework of sofas, apart from the short legs, disappeared under a fat layer of well-sprung upholstery. A typically Victorian emphasis on comfort rather than style is clearly seen in the Chesterfield, so named after the 19th Earl of Chesterfield. It was comfortable, certainly, and also extremely large. Rosamond Mariott Watson in *The Art of the House*, 1897, described it as 'about as comely as a gigantic pincushion'. Chesterfields of the early 20th century were smaller and quite pleasing to look at, especially when loose-covered.

Ottoman c. 1855

An eight-seater example of a piece with Turkish
ancestry. The ottoman as first introduced early in
the 19th century was a long low box, plumply
padded, something like a divan but shorter.
Circular and corner models with a central back
appeared in the 1850s, following the showing of
examples at the Great Exhibition of 1851.

Ottomans tended to be used in rooms which had
bow windows or circular ends and, as they still
are today, in picture galleries.

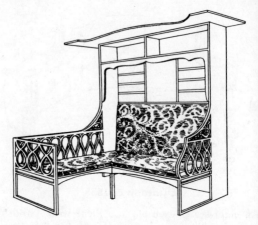

Cosy Corner c. 1896

The original advertisement for this piece read 'Solid mahogany Cosy Corner with well upholstered seat and back and covered tapestry, fitted with bookshelf, etc., etc.'

This type of flimsy wooden structure for filling the odd corner was sometimes made a feature of the late Victorian drawing-room or smoking-room. The shelves held all kinds of ornaments as well as books. Some cosy corners survived into the 20th century. Mostly, they were the product of decorating firms.

Round Music Stool c. 1830

One focal point of a typical drawing-room was the piano; it was lavishly encased, and the music stool to go with it had to appear a handsome thing. Stools with round adjustable seats were introduced early in the Regency period and were well liked for the ease with which they allowed the pianist to swing round and face his audience. Later there appeared on the market a type with a rectangular seat and a place below for storing music.

Loo Table c. 1840

The Loo table, named after a fashionable card game, was an important piece of furniture in both parlour and drawing-room, and large numbers survive. The grander ones were inlaid (an art in abeyance for case furniture and the bigger tables) and would be kept covered with a heavy cloth.

An early Victorian tendency to merge the various parts of a piece of furniture—rather as car-body parts were merged after the war—is seen above in the treatment of pillar and base, which are no longer distinct from one another. As with many Loo tables, the effect is by no means undecorative.

Victorian Work Table c. 1840

A piece evidently intended for games as well as sewing. The octagonal top lifts up on hinges to expose an interior divided into little boxes for sewing materials. The central compartment extends down into a tasselled bag, or pouch, made of the ubiquitous Berlin woolwork.

The table drawn is walnut. Its typically early Victorian base, heavy and imposing and ornamented with C-scrolls, reflects the sympathy of the period for the styles of Louis XIV furniture.

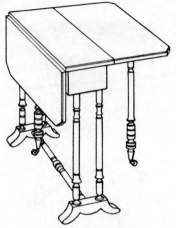

Sutherland c. 1855

A small table which might be called a cross between the early gate-leg table and the Pembroke. The main advantage of the Sutherland was that it could be made very slim when not in use; but it had no drawer and it tended to rock. The name was a compliment to the Duchess of Sutherland, one of Queen Victoria's Mistresses of the Robes.

In the example, it will be noticed that the corners of the flaps have been abruptly and arbitrarily chopped off where rounding would have been more pleasing to the eye. Victorian furniture often failed in matters of proportion.

Telescopic Table c. 1880

A dining table of solid oak or mahogany, to which extra leaves could be added. It was the most usual type in the late Victorian period.

These large tables may not be attractive, especially when fully extended, but they are comfortable to sit at and steady as rocks. Having the supports (generally bulbous and turned, as above) exactly below each corner, where no one sits, solved the problem of leg room more efficiently than had any previous type.

Arts and Crafts Table c. 1880

To give a small table eight legs seems excessive, but the furniture reformers of the late 19th century wanted at almost any price to make furniture different and more interesting. Chairs were occasionally made with five legs, two in front and three at the back.

This table, with its taut Gothicisms, is one of the more austere products, in oak, of the Arts and Crafts Movement. However, it does exhibit the painstaking craftsmanship which the movement set out to promote.

Occasional Table c. 1896

In an advertisement of 1896, this kidney-shaped structure was described as 'Quaint occasional table, of mahogany or art green, 37s. 6d.' In the nineties there existed plenty of similar bits of furniture. The fashion for cluttering up rooms with numerous tables was at its height, and the cheap furniture trade turned out a great variety of poorly made pieces vaguely in step with the designs put forward by the Arts and Crafts and Art Nouveau movements.

O

Sideboard c. 1855

Early and mid-Victorian sideboards made ideal vehicles for the admired mechanical carving reminiscent of the Louis XIV rococo style. The piece drawn, having enclosed shelves above, is more a cabinet, perhaps, than a sideboard; the most usual sideboard, always a display object, had a back-piece containing a looking-glass, a commodity which became a predominant feature in furniture from the 1840s when the mass-production of silvered glass began.

Wine bottles and decanters would stand on sideboards. Carving the joint was done at the dining table.

Large Sideboard c. 1860

In the 1860s and 1870s, and later, it was thought that art was something which could be applied to furniture to give it beauty; and a distinction grew up between 'art furnishers' and ordinary cabinet-makers. Carving was largely replaced by painted panels. Enthusiasm for mediaeval furniture (much of which had been painted) led to the appearance of all kinds of Gothic and Renaissance motifs, of which some may be seen above. The design of the piece illustrates a new emphasis on straight lines.

Early Victorian Chiffonier c. 1840

A piece considered appropriate for dining-rooms too small for the invariably obtrusive sideboard; it was also widely used as an enrichment for sitting-rooms. The example is a standard, fairly restrained, early Victorian type with its solid-fronted cupboard and two small shelves held by consoles to the backboard (the two Louis XIV consoles below the main shelf support nothing).

Later on, chiffoniers became more rounded in outline and gradually the backboard was replaced by a semi-circular looking-glass.

Whatnot c. 1845

Presumably it was the lack of a specific use for this piece—ornaments, books, music—which accounts for its undignified name (the French word is simply *étagère*). The whatnot has become a symbol of the fussy, over-furnished Victorian room, but in fact it first appeared at the beginning of the Regency period. The turning of the four posts was then restrained and elegant and often there would be a useful shallow drawer to each stage. In style, the example above comes halfway between the Regency model and the late Victorian. Whatnots became a standard furnishing item after about 1840.

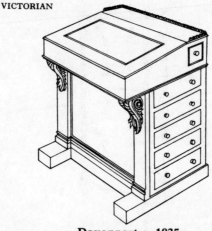

Davenport c. 1835

An invention of around 1830 which was still being turned out unaltered in the nineties. It especially pleased women, who used it for the writing of their many letters and notes and invitations. A merit of the davenport is the side-opening of the principal drawers which makes it unnecessary to move the knees when pulling them out. The top part, sometimes sliding forward on runners, contains a well, small drawers and, sometimes, secret compartments with hidden spring locks. The little desks got their name from the first customer of Gillows of Lancaster to order one. The record is still to be seen: 'Captain Davenport, a desk'.

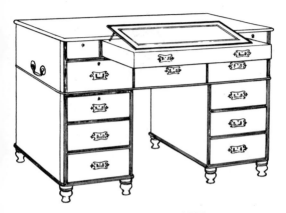

Military Desk c. 1835

A kneehole desk of cedar, camphor wood or mahogany, designed for travelling. It is in three sections, the top part merely resting on the two lower sections, and it has attractive, sunken drawer handles which made for easy stacking during transport. The feet can be readily unscrewed.

This functional piece is similar to the military chest of drawers—a piece of two sections. Both were being made up to the 1870s.

Fire Screen c. 1845

A decorative piece, introduced in the 18th century, which in Victorian times became a feature of almost any room in which a fire might be lit. The screen part, consisting of a panel of needlework or painted wood, usually moved up and down on its pole; this rested on either a tripod or a round base. When no fire was burning, the fire screen would be used to conceal the fireplace.

Victorian fire screens are as English as the coal fire habit; they hardly existed on the Continent where enclosed stoves warmed the rooms.

216

Early Victorian Wardrobe c. 1845

Wardrobes became, and continued, immense, and when they change hands today they are often sawn up to make two wardrobes, or simply for the sake of the timber, which is almost invariably mahogany. The plainer type shown above, with its boldly moulded cornice, achieved an impressively staid look in a large Victorian bedroom—and in the typical house of the period such rooms *were* large. Describing an inn bedroom in *Martin Chuzzlewit*, Dickens wrote: 'The very size and shape, and hopeless immovability, of the bedstead and wardrobe ... provoked sleep; they were plainly apoplectic and disposed to snore.'

217

Chest of Drawers c. 1850

One of the few Victorian pieces which tended to be simpler than its predecessors. Above is the standard type: two short top drawers and two fat long ones below. Cheap chests would be of painted deal, the more expensive of French-polished mahogany. Both sorts would have wooden knobs. The fitting of such knobs, often of the same wood as the furniture, began about 1800 and lasted some fifty years. 'They harmonise better and do not tarnish,' wrote J. C. Loudon in his *Encyclopaedia* published in 1833. Their introduction may really have had more to do with cheapness.

218

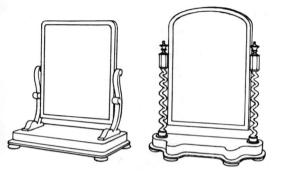

Dressing Glasses c. 1860

'You have baked me too brown, I must sugar my hair,' says Lewis Carroll's Lobster as he poses, in Tenniel's drawing, before a swing mirror almost exactly like the one here on the left. This was the most usual type of Victorian dressing glass and it would either stand, as the Lobster's does, on a draped dressing table, or on a chest.

Drawers in the base were no longer in fashion, but the solid mahogany slab made a heavy enough support. The dressing glass on the right, with its '17th century' twist-turned posts, was an almost equally common type.

Art Washstand c. 1870

In the 1870s painted tiles, wooden panels and vast wrought iron hinges were applied even to the functional washstand. It was felt that the more art, or ornament, given a piece of furniture, the more elegant it must become.

The piece drawn, more elaborate than most, is now in the Victoria and Albert Museum. It was painted by William Burges, a designer who was in the forefront of the Art Furniture Movement.

Quite humble washstands for a long time had had marble tops and marble splashboards.

Brass Bedstead c. 1885

Brass bedsteads came into fashion in the 1870's, and much trouble was taken in adding ornament to the plain brass rods, which were either round or in square section, as above. By this time the typical early Victorian fourposter, hung all round with curtains, was becoming a rarity; people were taking an interest in fresh air. Curtains were still used with the brass beds, but they hung from a tester which was attached to the wall or to the back of the bed and which extended only over the head and shoulders of the reclining person. Such beds were known as half-testers.

221

INDEX

WOODS ILLUSTRATED
ON ENDPAPERS

FRONT

ROSEWOOD	SATINWOOD
ENGLISH ELM	OAK
MAHOGANY	ASH

BACK

BIRCH	SCOTS PINE
WALNUT	BEECH
APPLEWOOD	YEW

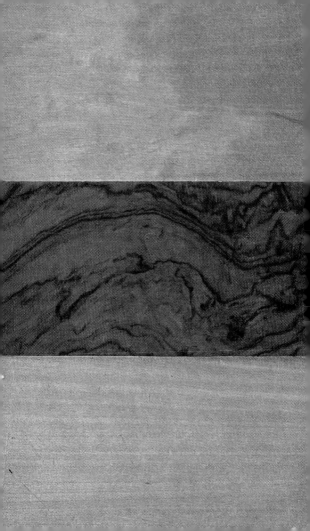